D1356228

Rural Women in Leadership

Positive Factors in Leadership Development

FSC
www.fsc.org
MIX
Paper from
responsible sources
FSC® C013604

I owe an immense debt of gratitude and love to my husband, Jeff McVay, and our son, Jack, for their patience and support during the writing process.

Rural Women in Leadership

Positive Factors in Leadership Development

Lori Ann McVay, PhD

www.cabi.org

CABI is a trading name of CAB International

CABI	CABI
Nosworthy Way	38 Chauncey Street
Wallingford	Suite 1002
Oxfordshire OX10 8DE	Boston, MA 02111
UK	USA
Tel: +44 (0)1491 832111	T: +1 800 552 3083 (toll free)
Fax: +44 (0)1491 833508	T: +1 (0)617 395 4051
E-mail: info@cabi.org	E-mail: cabi-nao@cabi.org
Website: www.cabi.org	

A catalogue record for this book is available from the British Library, London, UK.

Library of Congress Cataloging-in-Publication Data

McVay, Lori Ann.
    Rural women in leadership : positive factors in leadership development / Lori Ann McVay.
        p. cm.
    Includes bibliographical references and index.
    ISBN 978-1-78064-160-7 (alk. paper)
1. Women in rural development.   2. Rural women--Social conditions.   3. Leadership.
I. Title.
    HQ1240.M3594 2013
    307.1'412082--dc23

                            2013016573

ISBN-13: 978 1 78064 160 7

Commissioning editor: Claire Parfitt
Editorial assistant: Alexandra Lainsbury
Production editor: Tracy Head

Typeset by AMA DataSet Ltd, Preston, UK
Printed and bound in the UK by CPI Group (UK) Ltd, Croydon, CR0 4YY

Contents

Introduction

In April 2010, the European Forum on Women in the Sustainable Development of the Rural World put forth its recommendation for 'Promoting gender equality and the participation of women in the decision making bodies of key organizations in the elaboration, management and monitoring of rural development policies' (European Forum: The Role of Women in Sustainable Development of the Rural Environment, 2010). Five months later, a paper presented to the European Parliament in Brussels further highlighted recent focus on rural women as illustrated by the European Commission's concern with gender equality in developing the 2000–2006 and 2007–2013 Common Agricultural Policy (Bock, 2010b). This European context, rich with possibilities for the advancement of rural women, provided an ideal milieu for research into their leadership development.

Northern Ireland – with its vibrant rural communities and dynamic network of rural women's groups – supplied a rich localized site for this study. The six Rural Women's Networks in Northern Ireland – and an umbrella organization, the Northern Ireland Rural Women's Network (NIRWN) – provided a natural starting point for identifying participants, as their directors and other staff members fit well within the profile of rural women in leadership. And though not all rural women in the region are involved with the Rural Women's Networks, the networks actively promote the advancement of Northern Ireland's rural women at local, regional and national levels. This promotion is greatly needed, given the continued presence of gender inequalities and inadequacies in the areas of childcare, transportation, employment opportunities and training (Shortall, 2003; Rural Women's Networks, Northern Ireland Rural Women's Network, 2007). The networks, along with Northern Ireland's Department of Agriculture and Rural Development (DARD), have called for leadership development in rural areas as a crucial means of addressing these and other pressing issues. This study was therefore undertaken as a means of ascertaining the key factors facilitating the development and acquisition of leadership skills among women leaders from rural areas of Northern Ireland. Two secondary questions guided the research design. First, what people, organizations and/or events supported these women's development and acquisition of leadership skills? And, secondly, what thought processes and choices did they exercise in order to overcome obstacles in their development as leaders? As a matter of situating the study within current academic dialogue, research began with a review of pertinent literature.

Identifying the Gaps

An examination of sociological literature relevant to the topic of rural women in leadership[1] revealed several points of note. Much valuable sociological research has focused on rural women, particularly in the last fifteen years. Similarly, women's participation in organizations and leadership has also benefited from sociological research. However, the intersection of those topics – rural women in leadership – has received considerably less academic attention. Further, the studies that do exist focus primarily on obstacles and barriers to rural women's attainment of leadership positions. Such studies are crucial for their identification of negative factors that must be addressed. Nevertheless, they are also limited in their potential to positively impact the situation of rural women aspiring to, or serving in, leadership positions. For many of these women, this negative focus may contribute to a feeling of frustration. It leaves unanswered the question of how they are to address and overcome negative issues, and leaves unrecognized the existing resources with which to do so. In considering these points, two important gaps in extant literature become quite obvious: a low number of studies focusing on *rural* women in leadership, and a nearly complete lack of studies identifying and examining *positive* factors contributing to rural women's leadership development.

Addressing the Gaps: Conducting Research

This research addressed the gaps identified above in two ways: by providing insight into the developmental processes of *rural* women leaders; and – most distinctively – through the identification of *positive* factors beneficial to their leadership development. As noted above, the focus on positive factors provided a means of exploring the contexts in which rural women can – and do – overcome barriers on their journey to leadership. It also served as a tool for the recognition and affirmation of rural women leaders' powerful role as proactive change agents in their homes, communities and beyond. Interviews loosely structured around participants' life stories addressed the following areas: personal and community identities, family and community relationships, leadership role models and mentors, education, religion, and leadership experiences within organizations. In addition to inquiries into their personal leadership journeys, the women were also asked what advice they would give rural women aspiring to leadership, and what type of support they would like to see aspiring leaders receive.

Analysis

Analysis was undertaken utilizing the 'Listening Guide' as developed by Brown and Gilligan and expanded in the 2003 work: 'On the *Listening Guide*: A Voice-Centered Relational Method' (Gilligan *et al.*, 2003). In order to identify the Key Factors facilitating the development and acquisition of leadership skills among women leaders from rural areas of Northern Ireland, analysis of the women's narratives incorporated listening for the entire range of positive factors they voiced as significant. Because the 'Listening Guide' is a voice-centred relational method, each of the interviews was transcribed in the 'naturalistic' mode (Oliver *et al.*, 2005), including verbal starts and stops and vocalized emotional responses such as laughter and sighs.[2] Gilligan *et al.*'s method of analysis required multiple 'listenings' (2003, p. 159) to the transcripts in order to identify the various 'contrapuntal' (Gilligan *et al.*, 2003, p. 164) voices present in individual transcripts and to hear the relationships among those voices through the recognition of their points of harmony and dissonance.

Overview

Chapter 1 offers an in-depth review of literature germane to the current situation of rural women leaders in Northern Ireland. It opens with a discussion of gender identities, relations and roles from the broad perspective of women's studies, followed by a more narrowly focused discussion on rural women's experiences of gender identities, relations and roles, with special attention given to the unique position of farm women. The chapter then addresses organizations and organizational constraints to rural women's attainment of leadership positions. Subsequently, a brief sociological analysis of leadership is presented. This includes an overview of literature on women in leadership, and culminates with literature concerning rural women in leadership.

The methodological and theoretical underpinnings of the research are revealed in Chapter 2, including the details of the research design and profiles of participants. As a qualitative study, semi-structured, in-depth interviews were the primary method of inquiry. Participant observation provided insight into the cultural contexts of the women being interviewed, and the practice of reflexivity acted to highlight the researcher's voice as it spoke in dialogue with the voices of participants in the interviews and writing up of the findings.

The emergence of findings is rooted in two case studies (Alice and Doreen), presented in Chapter 3. These studies are representative of the full process of analysis. Beginning with Alice and Doreen's narratives, the presence of the Leader voice was identified in all twenty-two of the transcripts. This allowed for comparison of that voice across transcripts, resulting in the emergence of findings.

Chapter 4 begins with a discussion of External Factors in the participants' leadership development. This, and subsequent discussions of Internal Factors and Key Factors, provides context for the presentation of each of the factors, which is divided into three major segments: External Factors, Internal Factors and Key Factors. This chapter utilizes an emphasis on the participants' voices to define, describe and illustrate each of the factors.

The results of this study have significant potential to be applied practically, and to be utilized in the continued development of women leaders from rural areas. It is hoped that this book will be useful in both responding to and generating questions regarding the position of rural women in society and organizations, and that the findings will be of use to the growing body of policy makers concerned with supporting leadership development among rural women. As such, the book concludes with a summary of the findings and recommendations for further research and policy.

Situating the Study: A Review of Relevant Literature

Introduction

In the past two decades, sociological research in the West has witnessed a post-structuralist cultural turn that has opened new avenues of research to gender studies (Little and Panelli, 2003). Work influenced by this turn has not been received without criticism, particularly in the area of practical applicability (Cloke, 1997). However, the cultural turn's contribution to gender studies is evident in its rejection of any essentialist thinking that would lead towards masking differences between people of a given community (Little and Panelli, 2003). Thus, in order to properly introduce the context within which this study's participants experience their identities as 'rural', 'women' and 'leaders', this review of relevant literature begins first with a discussion of work from the broader realm of women's studies, narrowing to a more specific exploration of literature on rural and farm women. This is followed by a discussion of organizations and the constraints within which women operate in many organizational milieus, and an addressing of leadership as a sociological concept, including a discussion of the literature on rural women in leadership. Finally, the study is put into context with a portrait of women from rural areas of Northern Ireland.

1.1 Gender

1.1.1 Gender identities and relations

In embracing the resulting ambiguities of identity[3] construction and reconstruction that followed from the cultural turn, researchers have been able to uncover a spectrum of shifting – and even multiple (Saugeres, 2002) – gender identities formerly hidden within generalized categories (Bock, 2006). Biology is no longer considered the singular source of gender, with some feminist thinkers having labelled existing ideas of 'male' and 'female' as arbitrary (McCormack, 1993). Such labelling is understandable, given the fact that women's 'nature' has in the past been used as a source of domination by those who would claim that women's social roles are prescribed by biology and are therefore unchallengeable and unchangeable (Lawler, 1996).

According to Adrienne Rich, this biological stance has moulded society's expectations of women into unrealistic ideals of tireless caregivers to children and adult males (Lawler, 1996). Some feminist writers would lodge this expectation firmly in the realm of the family, noting it as a place where the facilitation of alternative gender relations is a near impossibility (Finch, 1996). According to Chodorow (in Crowley and Himmelweit, 1992), this situation is reflective of women's childhood relationships with their fathers (mediated through their mother, since fathers are remote), and exacerbated by the increasingly isolated nuclear family, which has diminished women's access to their sisters and mothers. Saugeres (2002) also writes that identity formation begins in early childhood (the very years in which many children are receiving the tireless care mentioned above). However, she notes that it is continually shaped through relationships by the recognition of difference between self and others. Further, McNay (2004, p. 177) posits that gender identities may only be recognized in the 'lived reality of social relations'. Thus, the formative role of relationships of all kinds is a particularly critical component in understanding the construction of gender identity (Brandth, 2002).

Rejecting the view of women's gender identity as biologically produced (and men's as socially produced), many feminists have come to name society as the construction site of gender differences (McCormack, 1993). Simultaneously, feminist scholars warn against going so far as to fictionalize the category 'woman', as such a deconstruction would 'deprive us of a position from which to speak as women, and a collective basis for struggle' (Jackson, 1993, p. 5). In a similar vein, Cosslett *et al.* (1996) write that the constructedness of identities in no way diminishes the reality of experiencing them – a reality that is often difficult for women to navigate, given the contradictory positions created by decades of equating the word 'person' with 'male' (Howell *et al.*, 2002). In response, a number of feminist scholars have embraced the concept of 'intersectionality', which requires inequalities to be examined as they appear across different social contexts and in relationship with the vast variety of women's lived experiences (Risman, 2004). Nevertheless, while women as individuals and in organizations have long fought against pervasive forms of domination, new forms emerge and become ensconced even as the old are torn down (Bartky, 1993).

1.1.2 Gender roles

In a social system where the domination of women is continually resurrecting itself in new forms, sex roles are produced and reproduced to reflect this dynamic (Sanday, 1993). With childbearing and child-rearing (nature/biology) still commonly viewed as determinants of women's proper social roles (Lawler, 1996), and housework and childcare still being performed primarily by women (even those who work outside the home) (Keith and Malone, 2005), it is a short leap to McCormack's statement that 'There would not be the social ferment over gender roles in Western industrial societies today if a substantial number of men and women did not subscribe to the thesis of universal female subordination' (Jackson, 1993, p. 85). Whether or not that thesis stands is a matter of contestation (Sanday, 1993). Nevertheless, women who mentally subscribe to feminist dissent against subordination may remain in exactly such a situation out of emotional commitment (Grimshaw, 1993).

In a 1993 study on women who worked full-time, Walby discovered this same attitude towards housework undertaken in addition to their outside work (Walby, in Henig, 1996). Despite the isolation of housework (as compared with the communal atmosphere of outside work, which many of them enjoyed), the women she interviewed not only viewed it as an expression of the love they held for their husbands and (in many cases) children, but saw it as appropriate for women to do this work and became defensive of their families when Walby attempted to broach the subject of their home workload. The women in Walby's study, by their outside work, stand in contrast to women who work exclusively in the home and accept that their efforts belong to a 'separate sphere' of work (Henig, 1996). Conversely, these same women who work outside the home still have both feet firmly planted in the domestic sphere, believing in the necessity of being solely responsible for the housework. This interaction between women's outside (paid) and home (unpaid) work has been described as the central concept in understanding women's experiences of being treated unequally to men (Truman, 1996).

Fourteen years after Walby's research, Cunningham (2008, pp. 1–2) described the results of a longitudinal study linking gender ideology and housework. According to the study's results, the second half of the 20th century saw an increase in the number of women in the labour force paralleled by a decrease in their household duties. Interestingly, 'their support for gender differentiated family roles' also fell (Cunningham, 2008). In linking gender ideology with participation in the labour market, Cunningham argued that women with egalitarian attitudes towards gender roles were more likely to have jobs outside the home and, further, to work longer hours than less-egalitarian women who worked outside the home (Cunningham, 2008). Additionally, women with young children were less likely to be employed (Cunningham, 2008). These occupational choices affect short-term job arrangements, but may have long-term consequences as well, since traditionally a long-term career is only offered as one continuous path of full-time employment leading to ever-higher levels of responsibility. Thus, women are often denied admission to the highest levels of organizations, regardless of their experience and skills (Truman, 1996).

Within the home, men's and women's tasks are still highly segregated (Keith and Malone, 2005). Women are often conscripted into similar roles in their outside work as well – caring roles that are unrecognized and unrewarded (Adkins and Lury, 1992). Even as women enter professional worlds such as law and medicine in increasing numbers, gender roles and inequalities transform to maintain themselves (Truman, 1996). In some cases this is played out to the extent that, even in similar (or the same) job positions, work requirements may vary by gender, with women being seen as less skilled and therefore given fewer opportunities to gain new and more valuable skills (Lawler, 1996). Not only is gender itself a factor in women's ability to gain new skills (and thus attain higher positions within organizations), but women's unpaid work may also cause them to make occupational choices differently from men – especially when a wife and/or mother's prospective job does not lend itself to easily accessible childcare and is not within an acceptable proximity of her unpaid work (i.e. the home) (Henig, 1996). Moreover, time spent in working in the home lessens wages – particularly for young and middle-aged women (Berik, 1996; Keith and Malone, 2005).

1.1.3 Summary: Gender relations, identities and roles

Issues regarding gender roles, relations and identities are present in all aspects of society, where they are produced and reproduced. Although feminism has brought many of these issues to light, this review of the broader literature suggests that most men and women continue to function in socially prescribed patterns. From this point forward, the literature reviewed will focus more specifically on the circumstances of rural and farm women.

1.2 Rural Women

The concept of a rural space has been defined in many and various ways. In seeking to avoid a loss of meaning of the concept of 'rural' altogether – and thereby a loss of place from which to speak in an active voice (Bell *et al.*, 2010) – rural sociologists are faced with quandaries similar to the ones (noted in Section 1.1 above) faced by feminist scholars in their use of the term 'woman'. While the rural community has come to be seen as a multi-faceted social construct with values defined by those who live there (Cloke and Milbourne, 1992), Bock (2006) observes that definitions of 'rural' are traditionally hegemonic and serve to reinforce power relations between genders. In spite of this, the popular image of rural dwellers as a close-knit, caring community persists, and expectations of finding such a 'rural idyll' not only draw people to rural areas to live but also serve to shape their behaviour while they live there (Little and Austin, 1996).

Rural sociology has come to look more and more to socially constructed gender identities as the source of men's and women's inequality (Little and Panelli, 2003). Present not only on farms, but in the broader rural community as well, is a persistent and pervasive image of women conforming to traditional gender roles (Silvasti, 2003). As an example of this, Brandth and Haugen's (1997) analysis of issues of the Norwegian Society of Rural Women's publication *NBK-nitt* from the years 1974, 1984 and 1994 reveals that, at base, the representation of women did not change. Women were safely portrayed as 'caretakers and farm hands as well as participants in the rural community'. In similar research, Morris and Evans (2001) considered the *Farmlife* segment of issues of the publication *Farmers' Weekly*[4] from 1976 and 1996, and noted that the passing of two decades resulted in a shift towards business-focused articles, but that little changed in the representation of a clear division of gender roles into the male/female duality, with women's businesses emerging as simply a commoditization of traditional household gender roles.

1.2.1 Gender relations in rural studies

The cultural turn in research also affected rural studies, creating interest in the role of communities in the production and maintenance of gender relations (Little and Panelli, 2003). Bock and de Haan (2004), in particular, note the close ties between rural gender studies and their sociopolitical implications. Gender relations, in this sense, are useful in revealing the cultural (as opposed to biological) sources of socially appropriate masculinity and femininity (Shortall, 2002).

Brandth (1995) noted in her study on masculinity and tractor advertisements that, even in the face of constant gender reorganization, male dominance remains firmly in place; and Silvasti (2003) writes that peasant communities maintain cultural scripts of patriarchy even as they adapt to meet the demands of modernization. Similarly, Saugeres (2002, p. 644) describes gender relations on farms and in rural communities as much more than a 'state of mind', but rather as ideologies reproduced through everyday activities – most of which remain patriarchal in nature. Little (2007, p. 853) links this to the 'policing' of sexual behaviours and the marginalization of non-heterosexual sexual practices within closely knit rural communities striving to ensure continuity in the values and morals they wish to reproduce. Five years after her study of *NBK-nitt*, Brandth (2002) attributed the male/female duality's persistence in society to its roots in structures and institutions that allowed it to be taken for granted as the norm and woven into discourses of all types. These discourses shape ideals of rural women, so that they are pictured as wives and mothers with no option of choosing the route of the single, child-free business professional (Little and Austin, 1996). Northern Ireland is no exception to this phenomenon, and, as a 2004 report on gender equality indicators testified, is actually more conservative in views regarding marriage than the rest of the UK (Breitenbach and Galligan, 2004). Interestingly, Little and Austin (1996) propose that many rural women actually deeply value the very characteristics of rural life that limit their choices regarding occupation and domestic duties, viewing them as simply fulfilling expectations as sustainers of rural communities.

Many rural areas may hold to a code of morality which places women's self-care and self-interest at the end of a long line of 'strictly proscribed' (and, at times, conflicting) duties of nurturance and care required by their family farm, family and/or community (Heather *et al.*, 2005). Women's acceptance in the community is determined by how well these differing gender identities and duties are carried out (Saugeres, 2002). This dynamic is made more complex by the fact that women's internalization of these expectations leads them to feel responsible not only for their own family, but for other members of the community as well (Little and Austin, 1996). In Northern Ireland, this dynamic has been reinforced by 'the Troubles' as women adapted to care for families during times when husbands and brothers were imprisoned (Women's Resource and Development Agency, 2008). Rural women may not recognize this as a form of subordination, but instead often label these expectations as simply an aspect of what it means to be part of a family rather than as gender roles (Heather *et al.*, 2005).

The subordinated position of women in rural areas can be attributed to a multitude of factors, ranging from long-standing ideologies regarding gender identities, relations and roles, to the decline in the economic stability of rural areas. Women in these communities operate in multiple gender identities, relations and roles, in spite of the obvious difficulty and personal cost involved in doing so. Although the rural community has come far from its days of being solely associated with farming (Bock and de Haan, 2004), the unique circumstances of rural women living and working on farms make it necessary at this point to examine more specific literature regarding their experiences.

1.2.2 Farm women

With the current economic upheaval in rural areas of many Western countries, numerous changes are taking place (Little and Panelli, 2003). Rural development policies have played an important role in these changes by serving to make farmers a minority in many rural areas (Saugeres, 2002). As farm wives move into off-farm work in increasing numbers, in order to support their husband's role as farmer, the effect on gender identities, roles and relations is evident (Shortall, 2002), but as the literature reveals, systems of subordination remain dominant and are compounded by the prevalence of 'masculinist approaches' to rural development policies (Bock and de Haan, 2004). Nevertheless, rural and farm women are far from powerless, as has been shown particularly in their successes as agents of rural development – in spite of opposition (Bock, 2004).

As with broader women's studies literature, the study of women and farming reveals the presence of a debate around women, society and nature (biology), which has led to claims that the association of rural women with nature has perpetuated male domination by reducing women to simply another feature of the landscape in need of male control (Little and Panelli, 2003). In fact, Brandth (2002), in a review of literature on gender identity in European family farming, noted that the research she reviewed clearly displayed the presence of a hegemonic discourse. The source of this discourse has been explored in varying ways, leading Delphy (1984) to write that farm women's relations rather than their actual work lie at the root of their exploitation as workers. Morris and Evans (2001) discuss ways in which hegemonic discourse is perpetuated by farm media. Shortall (1999) identifies the ownership of property as the fundamental issue. Silvasti (2003) notes the key role parents play in shaping children's attitudes towards the traditional rural way of life. Additionally, Heather *et al.* (2005) identify women as one key source of their own subordination, as they exercise agency in reproducing the very systems that oppress them – a concept supported by Bock's (2004b) assertion that farm women who took on entrepreneurial ventures would only continue to pursue those ventures if certain they would not interfere with their family and farm commitments.

Recent publications show that the majority of women on farms are still expected to be supportive of their husbands' occupation in any way necessary – even at the expense of their health – while at the same time being portrayed as in need of a man's protection (Bock, 2006). Kelly and Shortall (2002) describe how women contribute to this discourse through positioning their off-farm work as a 'family household decision' (p. 336), and viewing it as a means of ensuring their husbands' mental health. Likewise, O'Hara (1994) purports that women's work on farms is shaped through a series of negotiations that they make as to their priorities in relationship with the farm. Farmar-Bowers (2010) conceptualizes these negotiations as resulting from a sense of both personal responsibility to the family and the obligation to instil responsibility to the family in the next generation. Heather *et al.* (2005) attribute this dynamic to the deep integration of hegemonic discourses into the relationships between farm men and women.

Studies in at least six Western countries have shown that the unequal division of labour between men and women on farms is grounded in socially accepted definitions of masculinity and femininity (Bock, 2006). Morris and Evans (2001) claim that representations of masculinity and femininity that they studied in agricultural media echo this by showing a maintained gender division of labour even when women were central to, or equal partners in, business activities. This persistence in gender divisions of labour on farms has been influenced by the view of women's bodies and work as 'secondary' and inferior to men's (Saugeres, 2002), since it is done in the privacy of the home and is not as physical as men's work (Brandth, 2002). Women's work is thus made trivial unless it is done in direct support of men and their households (Little and Austin, 1996).

In fact, women's biological makeup is seen as not only a hindrance to their ability to complete the same on-farm tasks as men, but as an actual handicap that women may only attempt to overcome (for example, by becoming women farmers) at the expense of losing their femininity (Saugeres, 2002). In response, young women may turn to 'explicit and conscious performances of their femininity and feminine bodily appearance' at other times (Bock, 2006) in order to avoid being seen as inappropriate and therefore rejected by the rural community (Little and Austin, 1996). Just as the broader women's studies literature showed that job requirements might change with gender, so qualities of a good farmer may be rejected as bad when they are displayed by a woman (Saugeres, 2002).

In spite of the rise in women's off-farm work over the past several years, Kelly and Shortall (2002) found that women's household work and on-farm responsibilities have changed very little. Bennett (2004) confirms this in writing that patriarchy is alive and well on the family farm, with women still expected to handle the majority of domestic responsibilities. And even as Brandth (2002) discusses the possibility that women's off-farm work provides them with a framework from which to be seen as active in making choices that take them away from their subordinate position as invisible workers on the farm, she also consents that hegemony can still be maintained in the face of such changes. It is interesting to note, however, that rural and farm women are not always pleased to be re-enacting established patterns of gender relations. In Silvasti's (2003) study, she described the family farm as an 'ideological battlefield' on which traditional gender relations face the changes taking place in society at large (p. 162). It is important to keep these difficult intersections and experiences of hegemonic tendencies in mind as we now turn to the literature regarding organizations, setting the stage for a discussion of how gender and organizational issues affect women's attainment of leadership positions.

1.3 Organizations and Organizational Constraints

1.3.1 Organizations

It has been claimed that the foundations of classic sociology rest on the study of organizations (Parker, 2000). This is unsurprising, given the powerful status of organizations in industrialized societies (Perrow, 2000). Since the publishing of Weber's highly influential conceptions of organizational hierarchy and authority, organizational theorists have wrestled with debates of structure and culture within organizations (Hatch, 1997; Parker, 2000), striving to untangle the mutual influences organizations and society exercise upon each other (Scott, 2004). Most recently, this debate has begun to turn towards critical realism for explorations that reach past the limitations of postmodern and poststructuralist epistemologies (Reed, 2005). However, as with all 'new' perspectives, critical realism has met with critique (Mutch *et al.*, 2006).

Issues of gender within organizations have been studied productively for many years (Scott, 2004). Through these and other, similar, studies, organizational practices have been situated in the context of wider social discourses (Mills, 2002; Reed, 2005; Walsh *et al.*, 2006). However, current discussions of gender and organizations are addressing the assumptions of feminist studies on these topics, as well as asking whether gender can reliably be studied in the context of organizational culture (Mills, 2002). In part, this can be attributed to the movement towards a complex view of gender identities as multiple and shifting, in opposition to the traditional organizational studies' concept of organizations as 'naturally' occupied by men (Leonard, 2002). Mills (2002), while recognizing that women have made strides towards dismantling this concept, draws attention to the non-linear development of female advancement in employment. Similarly, Kreimer (2004) notes that women's entrance into the labour market has not significantly changed which jobs are available to women – clearly illustrating one of the ways in which corporations fail to allow wider social issues to affect their 'core business practices' (Westenholz *et al.*, 2006). Even after decades of affirmative action, many organizations are still struggling to integrate diversity in all its forms (Awbrey, 2007).

We must at this point return to the question of how such organizational practices are influenced by and simultaneously influence society (Scott, 2004), reinforcing (and being reinforced by) gendered practices. If we accept the definition of an organization as a group of people who are brought together by the requirements of a particular task, with different people performing various pieces of the task, then it is a small leap to recognize that the way in which the group is divided creates power dynamics (Hatch, 1997). Following on from this, it is also possible to conceptualize individuals as perpetuating existing power dynamics through social interactions (Reed, 2005). This resonates with leadership literature, which has begun to recognize such practices as contributing to the marginalization of women leaders through the failure of organizations with traditionally male-dominated structures to practically apply their own gender-inclusive policies and procedures (Elliott and Stead, 2008). Shortall (2002, p. 160) carries this concept into her research on agricultural and rural restructuring, and also finds in these fields the presence of gendered structures that 'support the status quo' by using inclusive language to mask an aversion to the process of *actually* addressing gender issues. These dynamics necessitate a discussion of organizational constraints faced by women, and, in particular, rural women in the process of attaining (and maintaining) positions of leadership.

1.3.2 Organizational constraints

It has been well established that women have a difficult time attaining positions of leadership in male-dominated organizations. Recently, this has been corroborated by a report from the University of the Highlands and Islands (UHI) Policy Web, which identified traditional attitudes about gender roles as a barrier to women's employment in rural areas (Shortall, 2006). Other frequently cited barriers are lack of accessible childcare and transportation, and the unavailability of stimulating and rewarding occupational choices – all of which work together to inhibit women's pursuit of careers and higher-level positions in organizations (Little and Austin, 1996). Once women are formally recognized as leaders in such organizations, the masculinized nature of the organization in which they are involved is unlikely to change, since the overwhelming majority of others involved are men (Shortall, 2001). Nearly every piece of literature on women in leadership addresses not only the obstacles women face in reaching positions of leadership, but also the many challenges they face during the time of their leadership (Appelbaum *et al.*, 2003; Greenberg and Sweeney, 2005 ; Trinidad and Normore, 2005).

For farming women, these difficulties frequently have their roots in the method of entry into farming, which most often comes through marriage and can dictate the extent to which they are able to be involved in decision-making bodies and practices (Shortall, 2002; Alston, 2003). Farming associations are facing increasing pressure as all-male organizations become less socially acceptable, but the positions to which women are given access are predominantly on subcommittees (Shortall, 1999). One particularly relevant example of this limitation in acceptable decision-making roles comes from Northern Ireland's Ulster Farmers' Union (UFU). It was not until 1996 that the UFU (founded in 1918) appointed a woman to their eighty-member executive committee. Interestingly, of the twenty-eight members of the UFU's Farm Family Committee, also established in 1996, twenty-three of the twenty-eight members were women (Shortall, 2001). Alston (2003) points out that, while groups such as agricultural boards often claim that appointment is based on merit, women are still routinely excluded from appointments, even when their education levels are higher than other candidates. Such exclusionary practices form what she has termed 'the grass ceiling' (Alston, 2003, p. 479). Other examples identified by Alston include: communities with 'particular views' of women, unlimited terms of leadership, unclear selection criteria and processes, the 'old boys' network' and a lack of commitment to gender equity (Alston, 2003, p. 479).

Pini (2003b) also touches on this subject when writing of the reluctance of mostly male agricultural organizations to elect women – even when their experience and qualification are recognized by the voters. Alternatively, one venue in which women have been able to participate more fully is in women's farming organizations. However, as noted by Shortall (1999), these organizations are labelled by gender (*women's* organizations as opposed to *farming* organizations), and the issues they wish to address are often kept to the periphery of male-dominated farming organizations' agendas. In Northern Ireland this is also true of rural women's networks, which, in spite of having a vibrant presence and role in rural communities, have met with continuous difficulties in obtaining long-term funding (Macaulay and Laverty, 2007). It is at this point that our review of literature brings us to the focal area of this study – rural women in leadership.

1.4 A Brief Sociological Analysis of Leadership

To facilitate the examination of leadership from a sociological perspective, it must be recognized that leadership studies owe a debt to Weber's concept of bureaucracy as a functional means of shaping employees into a coherent group of efficient service providers (Hatch, 1997). In fact, it is difficult to think of a more social act than that of leadership, since it could not exist without the relationship between a leader and her/his followers. Further, leadership is a dynamic interaction that appears in all societies (Hackman and Johnson, 2000). In spite of the fact that leadership literature abounds, however, authoritative definitions for the terms 'leader' and 'leadership' have yet to be widely embraced. Uhl-Bien's (2006) Relational Leadership Theory approaches the complicated discussion of leadership by differentiating between the study of leadership '*effectiveness*' and her focus on the '*relational processes* by which leadership is produced and enabled' (p. 667, emphasis in the original). From this focus, she calls for a more sociological examination of the contexts within which leadership develops. Elliott and Stead's (2008) study of a group of women leaders took such a sociological perspective, and concluded that this 'sociological lens' was better suited to explorations of leadership outside of the contexts within which it has traditionally been housed (p. 178). Postmodern leadership studies have thus seen the advent of complex and adaptable theories of leadership, creating a growing chasm between traditional positivistic definitions and 'new ideas about the nature of reality and of life' (Barker, 2001). Most recently, leadership has come to be understood as a 'moment of social relations', in which a group of people are moving towards a common goal, and during which leadership may appear in one of many forms (Ladkin, 2010).

1.4.1 Women in leadership

For many women, the exercise of entrenched organizational power has barred their access to positions of leadership. Barbara Pini (2005, p. 76) states: 'Scholarship on gender and organizations has demonstrated that both in definition and practice, leadership is intricately connected to the construction and enactment of hegemonic masculinity.'[5] In fact, Henig (1996) claims that, without the presence of women in leadership positions, even a significant number of women within an organization will not change the organization's treatment of women. In part, this may be ascribed to wider power relations that inform the perpetuation of traditional gender identities (Bock, 2006). This takes place in spite of the broader conceptions of masculinity and femininity now available to women (as the result of an increase in women's access to education and the labour market) (Brandth, 1994). In the language of discourse, women who attain leadership positions may be seen as resisting the dominant discourse by embracing an alternative discourse that flies in the face of hegemony (Bock, 2006). However, this does not put them *outside* dominant discourses and power relations (Jackson, 2004). On the contrary, occupations in which women are the dominant participants continue to be predominantly part-time, pay poorly and offer few opportunities for training and advancement (Kreimer, 2004). This often leads to a reproduction of traditional gender roles and identities in the workplace (i.e. few women in leadership positions), since organizational routines are not easily disrupted (Kreimer, 2004; Westenholz *et al.*, 2006). Recent theoretical discussions surrounding the positive value of so-called feminine styles of leadership (i.e. dispersed leadership or willingness to share leadership among a group) have served in some ways to reinforce the stereotype of women as motherly caregivers (Elliott and Stead, 2008). In this way, leadership continues to be housed within a quite 'narrow range of identities' standardized by organizations who fail to critique gendered assumptions underlying the norms to which they require their leaders to aspire and adhere (Ford, 2005).

1.4.2 Rural women in leadership

For rural women, this is also the case. Although among women's agricultural organizations women leaders have been more able to develop their own style of leadership, this style has yet to become acceptable among the traditionally male-dominated agricultural organizations (Pini, 2005). Practical issues such as childcare and domestic duties typically remain their responsibility and are often overlooked by the dominant male group when organizing meeting times and places (Shortall, 2001; Pini, 2005). Further, women in leadership may be expected to function as men while maintaining the appearance of femininity (Maleta, 2009). Such situations highlight the precarious position of women leaders, which requires them to be constantly aware of behaving in neither too masculine nor too feminine a manner – a quandary Pini has labelled as being a member of 'the third sex' (Pini, 2005). In many organizations, this is compounded by the fact that a woman in leadership is treated as a novelty, which limits her credibility and political power (Shortall, 2001).

Reed (2005) sees such gendered structures as existing prior to agency, and therefore acting as constraints to those who would change them, but also attests that these structures have continuous potential for transformation. In this way, he acknowledges the difficulty of an either/or mindset in the structure/agency debate, and creates a space in which women who operate within traditional organizational discourses may find room to make the arduous journey into leadership. Emirbayer's (1997) arguments concur, and go one step further by suggesting that factors influencing decisions can only be found by closely scrutinizing the many and varied social situations of the decision maker. McNay's (1999, 2003) approach to the limitations of the structure/agency debate align most closely with the objectives of this study in her recognition of the negative tone within much structure/agency discourse, and her proposal to include – within discussions around subjectivity – positive movements of creative freedom in which subjects may exercise agency in unexpected ways, rather than limiting it exclusively to negative or constricting conceptions. Given the divided history of Northern Ireland, it has the potential to be seen in such a negative light.

1.5 Contextualizing the Study: Rural Women in Northern Ireland

It is important to note that rural women often develop a sense of self that is inseparable from the context in which they are located (Heather *et al.*, 2005). Additionally, variations in the particularities surrounding the concept of 'rural' exist between and among rural spaces (Little and Austin, 1996). Therefore, although the women of rural Northern Ireland are not exceptions to the wider literature on women and rural women, it is fundamental to recognize the impossibility of generalizing rural women's experiences to women from all communities (Jackson, 1993), and to bear in mind that women from Northern Ireland will have interpretations of experiences and ideologies which differ from those of rural women in other rural locations (Little and Austin, 1996). One of the most unique facets of Northern Ireland women's experiences is that of the conflict which has been present in the region for many years and has served to heighten the role of women in the affected areas as nurturers and caretakers (Rural Women's Networks, Northern Ireland Rural Women's Network, 2007).

In 2002 (p. 161), Shortall wrote: 'the equality legislation that has emerged in Northern Ireland is far-reaching', but that 'the current face of agricultural and rural restructuring is not one that significantly advances gender equality.' Much of this can be attributed to the hidden undervaluing of women's representation that is present in Northern Ireland, as revealed in the lack of statistical information surrounding women's issues and the under-representation of women on rural development organization's management boards (Shortall, 2002). The following year, in her report on women in rural areas of Northern Ireland, she noted several specific issues facing rural women in Northern Ireland (each of which resonates clearly with broader literature): lack of adequate childcare, transportation difficulties, restricted job opportunities and limited access to training (Shortall, 2003). More recently, a 2007 regional report noted the continued existence of inequalities 'around labour market participation and pay, family and caring responsibilities, health needs, lack of representation at a political and decision making level, access transport, and violence in the home' (Rural Women's Networks, Northern Ireland Rural Women's Network, 2007).

Seeking to address these issues locally are six major Rural Women's Networks (Fermanagh, Mid-Ulster, Omagh, Newry and Mourne, Roe Valley, and South Armagh) and one umbrella organization (Northern Ireland Rural Women's Network, or NIRWN). These groups are led by women and are *for* women

(Crawley, 2005). They are often supported by, and work in conjunction with, the Women's Resource and Development Agency (WRDA) and Rural Community Network (RCN). In response to the above-mentioned issues, these groups and networks have, for many years, attempted to provide accessible childcare and training, but have continually met with difficulties in obtaining long-term funding and finding appropriate facilities and trained staff (Shortall, 2003). This can, in part, be attributed to a shuffling of responsibility for these organizations between the women's sector and the rural development sector, resulting in a lack of funding from both (Crawley, 2005). Thus, they have also experienced a change in focus from general development to specific projects (Rural Women's Networks, Northern Ireland Rural Women's Network, 2007). With the 2006 formation of NIRWN by the Department of Agriculture and Rural Development (DARD – a government agency), an attempt has been made to fit the previously existing networks under an umbrella organization as a means of coordinating their efforts. While this effort has met with mixed reviews (including questions regarding the motives for NIRWN's inception), rural women's networks continue to remain an active and essential part of rural life in Northern Ireland.

The six Rural Women's Networks and NIRWN responded to the European Union Programme for Peace and Reconciliation (Peace III) 2007–2013 plan by calling for a focus on building equality between women and men in three areas related to leadership, the facilitation of which should include provision for appropriate childcare and transportation assistance: participation in political and decision-making bodies, skills development, and giving women confidence to speak out regarding their political opinions (Rural Women's Networks, Northern Ireland Rural Women's Network, 2007). Similarly, DARD's 2007–2013 rural strategy promotes the building of leadership skills as 'a central pillar in the regeneration of rural areas' (Northern Ireland Department of Agriculture and Rural Development, 2006).

Summary: Intersection of this Study with Broader Literature and Research

In a 2005 article on the relevance of rural sociology, Beaulieu listed leadership development as one of the areas of inquiry that should be addressed in order to assure that rural sociology remains relevant to the fluctuating social make-up of the rural community. This provides an intersection for this research and the broader research on women in leadership and organizations. While there are authors who have ventured into the world of women in leadership, only a very few (see especially Alston, 2003; Pini, 2003b, 2004a, 2005) have concentrated their writings on rural women. This is particularly true in rural Northern Ireland (Crawley, 2005). There is a markedly noticeable gap in the literature regarding factors that positively influence rural women's leadership development. It is possible that this is the result of a conceptualizing of the rural community as a place where change may take place, but is not created (Bell et al., 2010). This work seeks to bring feminist sociology out of what Rosenberg and Howard (2008) have termed 'ghettoized spaces' (i.e. areas of sociological inquiry saturated by feminist work, to the exclusion of other areas) both by its identification of *positive* factors (in the form of people, events, organizations, thought processes and choices) that have helped to foster and promote women's development of leadership skills and attainment of leadership roles; and through its focus on *rural* women in leadership.

Introducing the Methodology and Participants **2**

Introduction

Because the methodology utilized in this study – particularly in the analysis of data – contributed in a unique way to the development of the study's results, the purpose of this chapter is to familiarize the reader with the methods used. A brief discussion of the rationale for choosing a feminist approach to the study is presented first. The research design, aims and objectives then precede individual sections on the data-gathering methods and the use of reflexivity. The method of analysis used to examine the data is addressed in detail, followed by profiles of the study's participants.

2.1 Feminism and Methodology

2.1.1 Why feminism?

Choice of method entails powerful, unavoidable consequences as related to the production of knowledge (Walby, 2001). Since – to many researchers – social science research is a social interaction which cannot be separated from its context (Lal, 1996), questions of knowledge production have been connected to calls for methodological choices to be made with a keen awareness of the study's social, political and historical setting (Stack, 1996). The challenges of these settings represent issues being faced by the entire social research community (Ramazanoglu and Holland, 2002). However, Letherby (2004) goes so far as to *centralize* within feminist research the choice of appropriate method in combination with implications of power relations between researcher and participant.

Bochner (2001, p. 135) asserts that, with regard to 'realms of lived experience' housing the production of knowledge, academia is merely one among many. One of the key ways feminism addresses power relations in knowledge production is through the recognition of women's experiences as a 'legitimate form and source of knowledge' (Pini, 2003a). This opens an avenue for exploring not only the individual women's lives, but other lives that may also inform the individual's experience. Thus, honouring the value of individual life experiences may allow the researcher to extrapolate insights to the larger social milieu and provide a means of working towards social change (Rosenberg and Howard, 2008). Because women's life experiences formed the foundation of this study, a feminist viewpoint seemed the logical choice in methodology.

2.1.2 What defines 'feminist methodology'?

The very term 'feminist methodology' is a contested one. In Pini's (2003a) article on feminist methodology and rural research, she recognized this, and attempted to reconcile her need for a methodological framework with the nebulous nature of a definition for 'feminist methodology'. In so doing, she puts forth five criteria that she adopted as her principles for conducting feminist research: '. . . a focus on gender, value given to women's experiences and knowledge, rejection of the separation between subject and object, an emphasis on consciousness-raising and an emphasis on political change' (p. 419). Pini's writing is thus representative of feminist concerns throughout sociology and many other disciplines, as each of these concepts continues to be in flux and the subject of academic debate (see, for example, McCall, 2005; Rosenberg and Howard, 2008), and so serves as a point of contact between my research with rural women and the broader spectrum of feminist research.

2.1.3 Challenges to feminist methodology

Choice of methodology provides no certain guarantee that the knowledge produced is directly connected to the reality being studied (Scheurich, 1995). Feminism is no exception to this quandary, which is compounded by the presence of myriad viewpoints on what does or does not constitute appropriate feminist method (Flax, 1987). Fortunately, this situation is not hopelessly irreconcilable, as the potential still exists for feminism to negotiate commonalities in the interactions between epistemology and politics in research (Walby, 2001). The basis for negotiation lies in feminist researchers' shared goal of gaining 'an *understanding of women's lives and those of other oppressed groups* . . . that promotes *social justice and social change* . . . and . . . is mindful of the *researcher-researched* relationship and the *power and authority* imbued in the researcher's role . . .', including how the researched are represented in the final write-up of research findings (Hesse-Biber, 2007, emphasis in the original), and the tangled process of how the researcher's subjectivities influence the knowledge she/he produces (Pini, 2004b).

Further challenges to feminist methods may be divided into two key areas, the first of which is the tension between dominant empirical approaches to research and research inclusive of women's experiences (Lather, 2001). Although theories of power are myriad among feminists, surrounding the shared goal of gaining understanding is the principle that knowledge produced by feminist research should in some way be connected to women's actual experiences of power within relationships – including those between the researcher and the researched (Naples, 2000). If we accept a definition of experience that embraces the multiplicity of activities involved in women's everyday lives (Brooks, 2007), it is understandable that experience as a valid source of knowledge has been criticized for a disconnection from theory, for lack of generalizability, and for the simple reason that the human senses are not infallible (Ramazanoglu and Holland, 2002). Nevertheless, feminist knowledge produced using experience as its basis has resonated strongly with many people, suggesting that the examining of experience within a rigorous sociological framework has the potential to produce findings that are both accessible and academic (Smart, 2009).

Secondly, incorporation of the poststructural concept of intersectionality ('the relationships among multiple dimensions and modalities of social relations and subject formations') presents quite a challenge to feminist researchers (McCall, 2005, p. 1771). This is particularly the case when varied ways of thinking (for example Eastern and Western) meet (Ramazanoglu and Holland, 2002). Feminist scholars have come to recognize that multiple positions on any given issue must be recognized – even when they are in disagreement with feminist thought (Pini, 2004b). However, this has also led to the assertion that discourse alone cannot capture the effects of experience on women's actual, physical realities, and therefore experience must be interpreted in some manner, rather than being merely investigated (Smart, 2009). This point brings us to the specific methods used in this study.

2.2 Research Design

Pini (2004b) argues that researchers interested in studying rural women are at a point in time that calls for a methodology which will, much like Sachs' (1983) work in *The Invisible Farmers*, make visible these women's hidden contributions. In light of this call, Shortall's (2002) view of the exploration of the farm household as key to research exploring gender roles and farm families' divisions of labour also seems appropriate to the broader rural community. This is not simply because farm women are an important segment of the rural population, but also because examining household gender roles is fundamental to the study of rural women in leadership. Furthermore, in spite of similarities in stereotypes of rural women, their experiences are actually quite varied (Little, 2002). Additionally, as Pini (2003a) points out, addressing issues from a localized perspective strengthens the feminist narrative by giving voice to 'women [who] have been marginalized and excluded by an all encompassing discourse of feminism' (p. 422). For this study, the household explored was chiefly the woman's childhood home (family of origin).

2.2.1 Aims and objectives

As set forth earlier, the aim of this research was to uncover factors that facilitated the acquisition and development of leadership skills among current women leaders from rural areas of Northern Ireland. Using qualitative methods rooted in feminist theories, this study sought to identify commonalities among women who are currently serving in elected or appointed positions of leadership. Wilkinson and Blackmore (2008) have noted that the majority of studies on women in leadership are institution focused – positioning women's development within the context of a particular organization. Rather than focusing on a single institution or contextualizing the participants' development solely in terms of a particular organization, this body of work attempted to address the women's leadership development as a social process rooted in their identity as 'rural'.[6]

2.2.2 Site

The first facet of research to be established was that of site. Because the focus was specifically on women leaders from rural areas of Northern Ireland, the rural women's sector in the region seemed a natural beginning point. Further interviews were conducted with women in other non-governmental organizations (NGOs), politics, business, churches and faith-based organizations, and agricultural organizations – types of organizations included in Macaulay and Laverty's list of rural women's groups and organizations in Northern Ireland in their 2007 'Baseline Study of Rural Women's Infrastructure in Northern Ireland'. Interviews with women serving in similar organizations outside the women's sector, were also included.[7]

2.2.3 Data gathering

In order to access a broad spectrum of women leaders' experiences, and to add validity to the study, two methods of qualitative data gathering were employed: in-depth interviews and participant observation. Simultaneously, reflexivity was utilized throughout the study as a tool for data gathering and also for maintaining awareness of any ethical dilemmas that might materialize (Buch and Staller, 2007). The use of semi-structured interviews following an interview schedule loosely contoured to the chronology of participants' life stories brought forward the types of experiences and thought processes participants considered valuable to their leadership journey. The study undertook an inquiry into rural women leaders' personal and community identities, family and community relationships, leadership role models and mentors, education, religion and leadership experiences within organizations. These facets of the women's lives provided starting points designed to spark discussion about their personal experiences of formative situations in which gender roles are often prescribed and traditional. From this perspective, these areas of inquiry also opened avenues of exploration into the complexities that surround women and leadership – particularly rural women in leadership (Rosenberg and Howard, 2008).[8]

In-depth interviews
Having established that the most appropriate form of interviewing for any qualitative study is dependent upon the research question, the methodology employed by Pini (2005) in her research into Australian rural women in leadership set a valuable precedent for this research. The use of general themes and questions as a framework for semi-structured interviews allowed Pini's participants to give self-reflexive answers about their own experiences as well as advice for aspiring women leaders. This study followed her example through the use of semi-structured, in-depth individual interviews – facilitating a more comprehensive understanding of the respondents' contexts and experiences in regard to the particular topic of leadership (Hesse-Biber, 2007).

The interview is a method that allows the researcher to maintain respondents' comments as valid and their experiences as valuable (Brewer, 2000), and helps steer the researcher away from forms of knowledge production that have come to be seen as patriarchal (Little, 2002). As such, interviews produced a wealth of rich data in the participant's own words (Brewer, 2000) and thus opened spaces that had the potential to reveal 'feelings, values and internal struggles' behind the stories told in the interview process (Ni Laoire, in Hughes *et al.*, 2000, p. 87). Reinharz and Chase (2002) recognize the hearing of women's own words as an antidote to centuries of their masking behind men's words, and put this method forward as particularly important when studying women. In view of the power struggles present in the experiences of women in leadership, this perspective was notably relevant to the research. Each woman was interviewed in depth once. The use of an interview guide helped ensure that the topic at hand was addressed, while also leaving room for the interviewee to articulate related issues or experiences that she considered significant (Kvale, 2006). The interview guide was adjusted slightly as themes emerged from interviews, producing continuity among the topics addressed and ensuring that the women's voices were reflected in the questions being asked.

Participant observation

Fundamental to my attempt to 'capture . . . social meanings and ordinary activities' as a way of deciphering how the women in this study make sense of their leadership circumstances (Brewer, 2000) was the practice of conducting participant observation at meetings in which they interacted with other women leaders from rural areas. Rural research has commonly made use of this method (Hughes *et al.*, 2000), and it has been described by LeCompte (2002) as an instrument for understanding broader cultural frameworks without masking differences among participants. Although it did not involve complete immersion into a field setting, early in the research I began attending meetings as a way of gaining acceptance among the women I studied (Brewer, 2000). This led to the recognition that their lives are quite complex and multi-dimensional – shaped by much more than simply their status and duties as leaders (Hughes *et al.*, 2000). It also informed my understandings of the role these organizations play in rural life and provided deeper insights into the participants' lives when they spoke about the organizations.

Particular attention must be paid to how much participation was appropriate to the setting (Buch and Staller, 2007). Wolf (1996) observes that research would not be undertaken if there were not existing differences between the researcher and the researched. Even in instances where the researcher shares some 'insider characteristics' with those being studied, it 'is not enough to ensure that the researcher can fully capture the lived experiences of those he or she researches' (Hesse-Biber, 2007, p. 141). Bourdieu (2003) attributes this to the foreignness of the researched group's formative practices and experiences as opposed to those of the researcher. While claims have been made for the advantages of both insider and outsider statuses (Wolf, 1996), much feminist research considers insider/outsider status as fluid (Lal, 1996) or, alternatively, views the researcher as both insider and outsider concurrently (Wolf, 1996). McAreavey's (2008) work gives further insight into the complexities of the researcher's overlapping insider/ outsider status through recognizing the continuous internal dialogue required to maintain both. This blurring of insider/outsider status was relevant to a point here, where my status as both an insider (daughter of a rural farm family) and an outsider (academic and native of the USA) informed my choices regarding participation.

Reflexivity

The common factor in both the interviews and participant observation was reflexivity. Reflexivity may be defined as a critical examination of the researcher's perspectives and experiences as they have the potential to influence her/his research (Fonow and Cook, 2005). Feminist research values the practice for its usefulness in revealing biases that help deconstruct researcher objectivity and shore up experience as 'a legitimate form of knowledge' (Pini, 2004b). It is also a key way of recognizing both similarities and differences between researcher and researched and among the researched as a group (Katz, 1996), and is particularly useful to researchers interested in women in leadership (Pini, 2004a). Reflexivity must be recognized and practised, however, as a critical process rather than 'a simplistic rendering of biography for its own sake' (Pini, 2004b) or an exercise that falls into the trap of being either too brief (and thus inadequate and ineffective) or too long (and thus narcissistic) (Bourdieu, 2003). Bourdieu (2003) sets forth the requirement that the researcher subject not only her or his experiences, but also his or her *relation* to those experiences, to meticulous scrutiny – recognizing that the researcher's location in the realm of academia will also influence research practices and outcomes. Unfortunately, in spite of the reflexive practices of feminist rural sociologists, reflexivity has had limited acceptance in the field of rural sociology (Pini, 2004b), placing it among the 'sociological subfields' Rosenberg and Howard portray as 'stubbornly immune to key feminist insights' (2008, p. 677).

Reflexivity is often relegated to the latter portions of academic studies. However, Hughes *et al.* (2000) advocate beginning the (continuous) reflexive process during the research design. Bourdieu (2003, p. 288) echoes Hughes by purporting that, without early reflexivity, researchers run the risk of 'injecting scholarly thought . . . into the behaviours of ordinary agents . . .'. Ramazanoglu and Holland (2002, p. 14) bring this insight to bear on feminist methodology through their recognition of the unfeasibility of compartmentalizing segments of our lives as researchers – the impossibility of separating academia from our 'everyday life' – and so admonish feminist researchers to be mindful of the social context within which we operate. Beyond introspection, Naples and Sachs (2000) expand reflexivity to include how the research is presented, choice of contacts, formality or informality in dress and speech, and the researcher's location during fieldwork – all for the purpose of exposing the process by which research conclusions have been formulated.

In the broader scope of sociology, Bochner (2001) embraces this element of research as humanizing the researcher, making space for the recognition of ways in which the research being undertaken is reflective of the 'therapeutic' and 'scholarly' intersections in our own lives (p. 138). However, this argument must also be tempered by Pillow's (2003) admonishment to avoid forms of reflexivity that build false connections between the researcher's life experience and similar (but not the same) life experiences of the participant. Pini's (2004b) observation that reflexivity has a constructive role to play in revealing the context of knowledge production in rural research (particularly when examining issues of power) necessitated the acknowledgment of my own positions as both 'privileged' researcher (Milbourne, in Hughes *et al.*, 2000, p. 179) and daughter of a farm family, among many others (see Section 3.1.1). To quote Pini (2004b, p. 172): 'The questions I was interested in as an academic were similar to those which plagued me growing up and in my roles as granddaughter . . . and daughter to farmers. I could not separate myself as the "daughter of . . . farmers" from myself as "academic", as traditional research paradigms would assert is necessary.' In so identifying her multiple subjectivities, Pini was able to reveal the ways in which they influenced her production of knowledge, and also to acknowledge the limitations of reflexivity in capturing the complexity of shifting and multiple researcher identities (Pini, 2004a). Similarly, I began by practising reflexivity in the design of this research, and incorporated reflection as an on-going part of the research. This continuous practice assisted in analysis, as it revealed relationships between topic, people, social circumstances and methodology (Brewer, 2000).

2.3 Analysis

2.3.1 Method of analysis: the 'Listening Guide'

Initially, analysis of data was to be carried out utilizing software. However, having carefully transcribed the interviews in the 'mode of naturalism' (Oliver *et al.*, 2005, p. 1273) – including verbal stops, starts and notations of emotional expressions such as sighs and laughter – the partitioning of transcripts required by the software proved unsatisfactory. A search for alternatives led to a method of analysis that much more closely aligned with the aims and objectives of this study, with feminist thought and with Brewer's criteria. This method – the 'Listening Guide' – was developed by Carol Gilligan and colleagues as a means of allowing multiple voices to emerge from a single interview, thereby revealing both the internal and societal (external) complexity of the individuals being interviewed and creating space for the reflexive voice of the researcher to be easily identified and to inform the analysis (Gilligan *et al.*, 2003). Mauthner and Doucet's (2003) recognition of the importance of reflexivity during analysis (as it stands alongside continuous reflexivity in the data-gathering phase) is reaffirmed by Gilligan *et al.*'s (2003) emphasis on the accessibility and identification of the reader/listener's voice.

The Listening Guide '. . . is centred on a set of basic questions about voice: Who is speaking and to whom, telling what stories about relationship, in what societal and cultural frameworks?' (Gilligan *et al.*, 2003, p. 159). These questions are pursued via multiple readings ('listenings') of the interview texts, with each reading focused on a particular aspect of the story being told. Gilligan *et al.* (2003) describe the steps as follows. The first reading (Step 1), is a listening both for the plot (including the speaker's social context) of the story and for the listener's response (including the listener's social context) to the story. The second reading (Step 2) makes note of the use of the word 'I' in the interviews – putting together 'I' (first-person) statements into lists called 'I-Poems'. This step is meant to draw the listener into the interviewee's life in a way that minimizes objectification of the speaker. The third reading (Step 3) is based on the musical idea of counterpoint, in which multiple melodic lines interweave to create a complex piece of music. As such, Step 3 involves listening for two or more voices within the narrative – voices that may either contradict or complement each other, but are nevertheless in relationship to each other. It therefore allows the reader/listener to recognize that one statement may have multiple meanings or reflect multiple voices on the part of the speaker, and that actions undertaken in relation to those meanings are reflective of the 'sense' the speaker makes of 'social existence' (Roberts, 2002). The exploration of the relationships between these meanings/voices is key to producing a rich analysis that is faithful to the speaker's voice(s). Additionally, this exploration assists in avoiding what Bridget Byrne (2003) refers to as the under-theorization of subjection resulting from neglecting to recognize relationships between multiple narratives. Its use in this study, in particular, contributes to scholarly debates through the utilization of Gilligan *et al.*'s (2003) method in examining the process of leadership *development* – an aspect of women's experi-ence for which her earlier work has been criticized for addressing insufficiently (Auerbach *et al.*, 1985).

It is important to note, in proceeding to the final step of the method, the presence of concerns regarding the 'soft', or 'feminine', nature of such methods in the writings of those who would place them over and against quantitative (or 'hard'/'masculine') research (Gardner, 2001). Gardner addresses these concerns via the mandate to apply a rigorous and thorough analysis that creates room for the presence of multiple voices, which here culminates in the final step of the Listening Guide (Step 4). Having 'listened' to the transcripts a minimum of four times, with detailed notes and markings being made each time through, the reader/listener revisits the original research question and asks the following: 'What have you learned about this question through this process and how have you come to know this?' and 'What is the evidence on which you are basing your interpretations?' (Gilligan *et al.*, 2003). Having asked these questions, the researcher then proceeds to bring each of the listenings back into relationship with each other, and – in exploring these relationships – to reveal the complexities of individuals' experiences in such a way as to produce a multi-faceted analysis that avoids objectifying the speakers or reducing their experiences to one-dimensional data (Gilligan *et al.*, 2003). This is especially important in light of methodological concerns regarding establishment of the veracity of such narra-tives (Gardner, 2001), and Byrne's (2003, p. 32) assertion that 'Not all individuals are able to present themselves at all times as coherent, whole subjects of a storied narrative'.

The voice-centred relational method proved particularly useful for analysis of the semi-structured interview data, in that it facilitated the hearing of narratives related to particular topics in unexpected places and in unexpected forms, intertwined with narratives relating to other topics. For example, in examining the women's accounts of their parents' community involvement, I had initially intended to limit 'community involvement' to participation in community organizations. However, it quickly became apparent that the women were telling highly relevant stories of community involvement in other contexts. A story from Gwen's narrative demonstrates this especially well. In speaking of her parents' livelihood as proprietors of a pub, and the sectarian bombing that had caused them to build a house separate from the pub (as opposed to living over the pub as they had before the bombing), Gwen related the following:

> It was always a mixed community, and our bar was always mixed. And my parents would have influenced me very strongly too. A lot of the locals would have been outraged by [the bombing], and very supportive. And certainly, my parents always gave us a message about being non-sectarian. Everybody welcome, regardless of what- w- I grew up with a strong, I suppose, a- a sense of being Irish myself and my family, but equally, people came in, that, you know, w- would have seen themselves as British. And, and whatever. And that wasn't a problem. It was just- Because it was the local pub, it was just a very much a focal point in the community.

In this particular narrative, it becomes apparent that she is not only speaking of her parents' leadership roles as business owners, but also their commitment to fostering a welcoming cross-community space. This example clearly illustrates the nuances found in each of the transcripts, as participants' responses to questions at times housed multiple, shifting contexts and layers of meaning in relation to the study topic (Pini, 2004b). Two case studies are presented as examples in Chapter 3 to demonstrate the full process of this analysis and the quantity of rich data it produces.

2.3.2 Limitations of analysis and representation of participants

Although the researcher may speak with some authority in the writing up of the analysis, it is vitally important to the validity of the study that the researcher also admits to the limitations of their perspectives and portrayal of the reality of the research field (Brewer, 2000). Rural research has come to embrace similar criteria as the importance of reaching 'shared understandings about a topic' between researcher and researched has grown within the discipline (Hughes *et al.*, 2000). In the words of Pini (2003a, p. 422): 'It is not the method we use, but how we use the method that gives value to women's experience'.

2.4 Participant Profiles

In order to provide a context facilitative of an informed and relational hearing of the women's accounts of their 'lived reality' (Jack, 1991), it will be helpful here to profile the range of social locations that they occupied (Emirbayer, 1997). These profiles are drawn from the women's responses to the interview questions, and so broadly adhere to the contours of the interview schedule beginning with participants' identities as rural/woman/leader and continuing from their families of origin to the subjects of religion and church involvement, educational experiences, extracurricular activities and leadership opportunities.

In the final step (Step 4) of Gilligan *et al.*'s 'Listening Guide' (2003, p. 168), the listener is instructed to 'return to the research question that initiated this inquiry' and ask what she or he has 'learned about this question through this process'. In revisiting this study's primary research question, it became apparent that listening to the women's verbalizations of themselves as rural, as women and as leaders was primary to any discussion of their leadership development. Bearing this in mind, a summary of the ways in which participants identified themselves as 'rural', as 'woman' and as 'leader' is presented below.

The women's articulations of their identities as 'rural' and 'woman' were often less formal than their articulations of the definition of leadership and how they saw themselves filling (and/or not filling) that role. In part, this can be attributed to the directness of the questions I asked regarding their definition of leadership and fulfilment of the role of leader, as opposed to the more generalized discussions of the subjects of rurality and womanhood dispersed throughout the interviews. This may also be partially attributed to their comfort level in self-identifying as 'rural' and 'women' (which appeared as well-defined concepts in their narratives) and the nebulous nature of the definition of leadership. Nevertheless, clear articulations of their self-concepts in all three areas emerged as they narrated their lived experiences.

2.4.1 Identity: Rural

> I will always say that my, um, the fact that I was brought up in a rural community, that I've chosen to live there and bring *my* children up in a rural community, it's very much part of my cultural identity. Um, and the, and, the **fabric** of my culture and identity. It's another layer.
>
> -Barbara (emphasis hers)

> But, if you're asking me, I'm a peasant woman. And proud of it. And I, I love, eh, rural Ireland.
>
> -Eva

The centrality of rurality to many of the women's concepts of self is clearly captured in the two statements above. In accord with the work of Mahon (2007), which suggests that having one widely accepted definition of 'rural' is not as important as the lived experience of the person speaking about the concept, participants' individual identities and perspectives resulted in the voicing of many versions of 'rural' in their narratives. For Joan, rural meant 'small town':

> [It] was a small town. About, um, twenty-five mile, thirty mile from Belfast. Called [town]. And, half there and half in [another town], which is an even smaller town. A further five mile on. And so sort of one-street towns. And, living on the outskirts of those.

For Maureen, it meant 'the country':

> Yes, I grew up in the country. I grew up beside [a lough] – the western shores of [the lough]. Um, we lived about, maybe a mile and a half from the lough. Where I live now, I moved five miles down the road, but I'm nearer the lough now. Um, we had a country upbringing.

Sara's concept of rurality included a mixture of town and farm references:

> My family were farming, a farming family. . . . Daddy, me father, didn't work outside, none of my parents worked outside the home. The farm was their main source of income . . . Yes, we lived- [name of place]. Which is a small townland. Um, it's about fifteen miles from [larger town]. Um, we have a primary school and a post office, but that would be about it, in terms of services. Um [town] would be the nearest town, and it would be four miles away.

And, finally, Olivia and Patricia both defined 'rural' in terms of farming:

> O: Well, I grew up in rural [county]. So, we lived on a farm . . . When I was very little, I can remember, sheep, cattle and pigs and hens on the farm, as well as beef cattle. But, gradually then, it became an all-beef farm. And that's what it is now, with my brother still on the farm.

> P: I grew up on a farm as well. South [county]. Um. It was, quite a small farm. . . . And we had pigs. But, like Olivia said there were always, hens, and, maybe a cow, and milk, and then, a goat. Which, I usually had responsibility for [laughs]. And things like that around the farm as well. Um. But i-it did become more intensive. And certainly, say the number of sows, for example, would have been, been built up, built up, and, the age at which the pigs were weaned would have been reduced. And I would have been very much aware of all of those issues. And very much involved, in all of those issues. Um. R- really, growing up on a farm, you had to do all those things.

Not all of the women were as vocal as Eva and Barbara in identifying themselves as 'rural' (see quotes at the beginning of this segment). Nevertheless, many of the participants' narratives conveyed a similar love of place, thus strengthening claims purporting that identities are contextually specific (Bock, 2006). This was especially true of the narratives in which being from a rural area was not singled out as an extraordinary fact, but rather as normality, as with Irene: 'I grew up in [small town], in the country. . . . Always kind of in the rural. I always kind of stayed close to home.' For Veronica, it showed in her account of having to leave her rural home in order to obtain a job promotion:

I did live in a rural area up until two years ago. But if I really wanted to follow promotion and if I really wanted to get to, I'm middle management in this organization . . . If I wanted to get [to] **that** level, I had to leave my area. You know. Um. There aren't that many promotional opportunities for women in rural areas. . . . And, and that's a bit of a disadvantage. I couldn't have this job without moving to the city. And that's regrettable. For rural women. For rural society. For, rural development. That's a bit regrettable.

Regardless of the differences in terminology and concepts used to define 'rural', each of the women's narratives reflected the indelible impact of the 'rural' on their lives and personal identities. As will be shown in the next section, these rural identities connected in fascinating ways with their identities as women.

2.4.2 Identity: Woman

Well. Don't, don't try to be a man, is one thing. I mean, and that's something that I would have fought very hard because as I said I was very much right through working in a man's world. Even down to the fact I **refused** to get dressed up in a navy pinstripe suit. I thought, 'I'm not doing that!' [laughs] . . . But probably as I got older, I *always* wore a skirt. And I made a point of doing it. 'I'm not going to come in here as the, you know, sort of, [laughing] half-man type person wearing pants.' So, I mean, even wee things like that, I refused, I refused to to be turned into into a man. And I mean at times, I mean whenever they would have been debating things- I mean [I] feel I was coming from a female point of view. And I do think women have a different way of looking at things. And I would have said that. I think you need both. I mean, I'm not- And that I suppose is another thing. Don't try to do men down. They are human beings. They have their points of view. They're coming at it from a different point of view. Try and work with them – as human beings. I, I, I always feel very uncomfortable when I'm with other women and they just start getting at men. I don't think that's on.

-Katherine (emphasis hers)

As illustrated appositely by Katherine's words, the robust and intricate junctures at which these women's distinctly rural voices intersected with others of their voices in addressing issues of gender identity and/or what they perceived as feminist issues confirmed Little and Panelli's (2003) declaration of the rural as a source for generating original concepts rather than as simply another subject for examination within current theoretical frameworks. Despite their concerns regarding the place of women in society in Northern Ireland, many of the women were quite concerned that they not be viewed as feminists[9], and brought that point to my attention with no prompting or direct referencing of feminism on my part. Sara provided a further illustration of this uniquely complex intersection of viewpoints. Although she spoke with conviction about the negativity of the Catholic Church being '*so* male-orientated and dominated' (emphasis hers), the very word 'feminist' elicited from her a tremendous reaction:

And I would say as well, I've had exposure to, feminists, you know. And- I don't li- I don't, you know- Better watch what I say, I suppose. But it just gives me images of militants and going out and burning your bra and stuff. And, even- funny I was reading something came in the post to me from the WRDA – Women's Resource and Development Agency – and, I was reading their mission statement and or, or some of their stuff in their new brochure. And it said they come at it from a feminist perspective. And all of a sudden I was going [makes shuddering noise]. You know, because, I don't see myself as a feminist. I see myself as a, a family woman, as a mother. As a worker. And- Maybe feminism is too much of a challenge for me. [laughs]

Sara's identification of herself as 'a family woman, as a mother. As a worker' holds true to literature that suggests rural women are concerned that they be viewed in the rural community as nurturing and caring (Saugeres, 2002; Heather *et al.*, 2005). Her frustration at the lack of women in leadership in her faith com- munity (a situation likely to be identified as problematic by feminists) was later followed by her reassertion that she abides by traditional roles, suggesting a complex dance between identifying with feminist ideals and rejecting the label 'feminist'. However, even in this complex dance, she demonstrated confidence through continuing to express her opinion at the risk of offending me ('Better watch what I say, I suppose') and also by speaking against an organization that supported her work in community development. In so choosing to confidently speak ideas that resonated with feminist thinking (albeit not under the label 'fem- inist') *and* to positively assert her identity within the rural community in roles that could be perceived by feminists as oppressive, Sara represented several of the women in the study who embodied Shortall's (2008, p. 452) view of non- participation (here in feminism) as a 'valid and legitimate choice . . . made from a position of power'.

Sara was not alone in characterizing herself as filling traditional roles, nor in her rejection of the label 'feminist', nor in recognizing the male-dominated nature of many organizations present in rural areas. Margaret – who echoed Sara in asserting 'I'm not a feminist' – went a step further than Sara and embraced her identity as 'woman' as a means for change, although housing it safely within the language of service to family:

> I was, um, involved in [large farming organization]. It's- it's very much a male organization . . . I was invited by the [then-President] to head up a working group to look at ways of getting women involved in the [organization]. Because what was happening was, the women were doing the work behind the men, the men went off to the meetings and the [laughing slightly] women were doing the hard work at home. [laughs] . . . And we gathered ten people from across the province and it took us about a year, but we eventually persuaded the [organization] to set up a farm family committee. And I then served on Executive as, I was made Chairman of that committee.

Niamh's bold feminism stood in stark contrast to Sara and Margaret's tradi- tional expressions and their position in the literature on rural womanhood, as she advocated education on the feminist evaluation of women's position in society for the development of future rural women leaders:

> Women have suffered so long from internalization, and I see it every single day. They have internalized everything from body image to, you know, th- their lack of ability. All that kind of stuff . . . [W]e have designed a course through [university] for the community activists, and have looked at feminism, misogyny and the light bulbs are going off all over the place. And you know that it may cause marriages to break up, families to break down. . . . And people are worried about that and the changes that that consciousness-raising, um, you know, causes. But, not only training, but it's mentoring . . . it's for women to be able to talk about that. And, not to get involved in backstabbing and bitching the hell out of each other.

It is interesting to note that even Niamh, by far the most unabashedly feminist of the women I interviewed, embraced a tone of care in her narrative. The difference between her focus of care (the women themselves) and the focus of care in other participants' narratives (family and/or community) set her at odds with traditional views of gender in rural communities (e.g. Heather *et al.*, 2005; Bock, 2006). Fascinatingly, the overarching marker of identification as 'woman' among participants who either identified with *or* rejected the label 'feminist' seemed to be the capacity to express that care for others in some active form, rather than any purely biological construct (Little and Austin, 1996). It is at this point of actively demonstrating care that rural women were most readily able to recognize their role as leaders.

2.4.3 Identity: Leader

> I think, how I would define [leadership] and what's appropriate to a community or to a society or even to a nation changes with time. And I think that at the moment, we're in an era of, you need to have personal power. You need to have a self-confidence. And, a lack of ego. And you need to have, um, an openness. Uh. And a humility. Um. That hallmarks the modern leadership era.
>
> -Veronica

> I think a lo- for a lot of women, they don't see themselves as leaders but they clearly are, uh, within their, uh, respective groupings and whatever they're doing. . . . I would give them the advice not to think of leadership in [a] boxed way. Um, so to think of leadership in the widest possible way and, and to work through- I mean if I said to a group of young women from a rural area, 'You're all leaders,' they'd go, 'Aye right. Dead on.' [laughs] But most of them probably are. Um, whether it be in school or in their church or in their community or whatever. So, it, it's getting people to think about leadership in a different way.
>
> -Cara

Veronica's astute observations on the nature of leadership combined with Cara's willingness to consider 'leadership in a different way' encapsulate the multi-faceted and problematic term 'leadership' as conceptualized, voiced and lived out by the women in this study. It was noted earlier that there is no widely accepted, all-encompassing definition of leadership. As with the universe of literature addressing various forms of leadership and its elusive definition (see e.g. Barker, 2001), the ways participants defined leadership also covered a broad spectrum. For some, it meant highly visible and difficult-to-attain positions with which they felt little identification. This point of the spectrum was exemplified by Olivia's words: 'I guess the initial reaction is those big positions of power. World leaders and that kind of thing.' For others, it was defined though their earliest experiences of leadership, which were often downplayed. This was the case for Fiona, whose views illustrated the opposite side of the spectrum (emphasis hers):

> Um, I suppose being the second of fourteen, you know, maybe it was sort of, ummm, understood we did look after the rest of the children, bring them- you know, rear them [short laugh] as well and everything. So I suppose myself and my older sister **were** the leaders in our family, I think.

For many of the women, leadership and responsibility were closely linked, if not equivalent. The use of phrases such as 'get on with it' or 'it just needed to be done' or being 'willing to do something' (as opposed to not taking action to meet a perceived need) reflected that link and demonstrated the matter-of-fact attitude that had led to their taking up of leadership roles apparently (on the surface) by default rather than out of an active pursuit of such a position. However, a deeper examination of the women's narratives revealed that leadership skills were often present and in use in some way prior to their 'default' appointment or election to a leadership role. Therefore, for those women, 'leader' seemed to exist as a position or title outside their self-concept until they were identified as such by others and then internalized the concept through living out a specific leadership role. Maureen's discussion of her early leadership experiences reflected this thought process clearly, as she realized, 'Well if I don't do this . . . nobody else is going to attempt it', and self-identified as someone 'who [was] going to do something. Like, rather than people who, just, didn't want to do anything.' Margaret, in spite of recognizing the valuable work she had done during her time serving as a local chairperson, described her experience in becoming the president of an international women's organization in terms of surprise, downplaying the successes of her leadership at the local level:

> And then, uh, on my- in my second term on the Executive in Belfast, I was made, uh [organization] Chairman . . . And during that time, we, uh, reorganized the areas, and we wrote a new constitution! . . . And then, when I was [Chairperson], in that role, that then, it said that I had to go [to] the world meetings of- the meetings of the world organization . . . to represent Northern Ireland. Well, again, I was a very small cog or a- in a wh- big wheel, or a [slightly laughing] very small fish in a huge pond. All these very important women who seemed to have lots and lots of things to say. And when I went to that meeting I could never have dreamed that one day I would be World President. I went along. I was fascinated by the work that they did. And I found myself, uh, being invited, eh- the second time I was there representing

Northern Ireland, to chair a workshop. Not that I'd done anything exciting at
the first time, but I think they just saw a young face and thought, 'Get her'.
[laughs] I-I-I think that's probably what did happen.

Tracy, who held a public office, showed a different facet of this type of
experience:

Have to say, Lori, when I got involved in politics it wasn't to be elected. My, my
whole reason for begi- for becoming involved in politics and for, for doing what
I did, was to help . . . And, you know, whatever the party asked of me, I was
prepared to do. . . . I was there to do my bit-

While some of the women demonstrated this attitude of minimization in
their narratives, others had embraced leadership – and the identification of themselves as leaders – boldly. However, even that boldness was tempered by a continued recognition of the importance of people and relationships. Gwen articulated
this concept by relating leadership to people and management to tasks:

Well leadership is about bringing people with you. Having inspiration and
vision, and bringing them with you. I mean there's obviously management bits
to it, but it's, you know, they're two different things.

Barbara also clearly presented herself as a leader, and, also like Gwen, distin-
guished leadership from management in a way that gave priority to people and
relationships:

I- I'm feel very fortunate that I have a very strong management team in the
division. So, I tend to be very very clear what is required. And what the end
game is. What, what the results would like them to be. Have a discussion with
them as to how they get there, and then I let them, manage it. And I will, um, I
will only step in if I think we're losing sight of the end game. Or, we're losing
time. Or we're not spending our budget properly. They're the three times I
intervene. And by and large in feedback I've got from the management team,
they're all- Think it's *really* important to give feedback. Um. But they say I
know when to step in and I know when not.

The range of leader identities among women in this study was reflective of
broader discussions attempting to definitively describe leadership as a concept.
However, as with their identities as women, participants' unique perspectives of
leadership articulated a desire to act in ways that would positively impact the lives
of others.

2.5 Profile: Families of Origin and Present Family Structure

The majority of the women identified their families as 'working class' or 'comfort-
ably off'. All of the women came from rural areas of Northern Ireland, and
nearly half were reared on farms or in close connection with farms belonging to
extended family members. The 'overwhelmingly White population' (Connolly,
2005) of Northern Ireland was reflected in the sample make-up: all of the

participants were white. Two of the participants were the only children in their home. The rest came from families of two to fourteen children. Of those who had siblings, six identified themselves as the eldest child, and four as the eldest or only female. Only one of the participants identified herself as further down in the birth order, being the eighth of ten children. Nearly all of the women came from traditional two-parent homes; and all but two were from homes in which the parents shared similar religious backgrounds. Two of them identified their parents as having a 'mixed' (Catholic/Protestant) marriage; two others' parents' relationships had 'broken up' or 'split up'; and one woman's father had died in her teen years. Over half of the women identified themselves as married at the time of our interview, two additional participants stated that their marriages or long-term relationships had ended, and more than half of the women had children.

2.6 Profile: Religion and Church Involvement

The women in this study came from varying Christian backgrounds, with nearly an equal number coming from each of the predominant traditions of the region (Protestant and Catholic). All but one of the participants described their families as facilitating participation in church activities. Approximately one-third of the women specifically noted involvement in Sunday School, some both as attendees and later as leaders or teachers. Fascinatingly, a preponderance of the women had – at some point – challenged or disagreed with the teachings of the faith tradition or congregation in which they were reared. Of those who spoke openly about their adult or current involvement in the church, four stated that they had completely left the church as an organization and seven noted that they were still involved in activities ranging from attendance to leadership.

2.7 Profile: Educational Experiences

Nearly all of the participants had attended small, rural primary schools. However, their further educational experiences were widely diverse. More than half had attended an all-girls school at some point in their schooling process, and all had at some time attended a mixed male/female school. Six participants specifically mentioned sitting for the 11+[10], five pointed out their attainment of O-levels, and eight noted A-level achievements. All but four of the women had attended university, achieving degrees in an assortment of subjects. Several had postgraduate degrees as well.

2.8 Profile: Extracurricular Activities

Involvement in an assortment of organizations appeared throughout the women's narratives. Guides, Girls' Brigade and Young Farmers were the predominant community and religious organizations cited. Nearly half of the participants had taken part in sport teams, several serving as captain or chair of those teams. A quarter of the women had travelled and/or lived internationally. Participation in community organizations, youth clubs, music, drama and volunteering were also mentioned by a number of the women.

2.9 Profile: Developmental Leadership Opportunities

In profiling leadership opportunities that helped shape the women into the leaders they were at the time of our interviews, it will be helpful to bear in mind that the paths taken by the participants on their journeys to leadership created a unique narrative for each of them. Although many shared experiences, none of their expressions of leadership or choices regarding leadership was identical. Thus, this profile is a broad overview of the most-common experiences of leadership among this particular group of women. Of all the leadership activities undertaken by the participants in their childhood and teen years, serving as Prefect or in a related capacity in their school was the most common, with leadership of a sports team following closely behind. Leadership in Guides, student government bodies, Sunday School and Young Farmers were also cited. As adults, the women's leadership experiences broadened to incorporate organizations not only in Northern Ireland, but across the globe as well. Additionally, formal leadership training had been a part of more than half of the women's leadership development. One of the most interesting facets of their leadership journeys was that many of the women had at some point been in leadership with organizations outside the field in which they were involved at the time of our interview. Six of the interviewees were serving in public (elected) office, three in private sector policy/development organizations, one as an academic researcher, three at rural women's networks or centres, one with a young people's organization, three in business, three in a public research/development agency and two with women's religious organizations.

Summary: Participant Profiles

Participants came from a diversity of familial backgrounds. However, all participants had some degree of religious involvement – whether in the past or present. Educational and extracurricular activities factored significantly into each participant's leadership development, along with opportunities for leadership experiences. Although in agreeing to participate in this study, the women self-identified as 'rural women leaders', the concept of 'rural' was expressed slightly differently by each of them. Participants seemed more unified in their identities as women, with care for others being that identity's hallmark. Leadership was also characterized as a role in which care for others could be manifested (although this seemed to stem more from the lack of a clear and unified definition than from a simplification of the concept), and with which the participants identified to vary-ing degrees. For the women who participated in this study, being 'rural', being 'women' and being 'leaders' meant many different things. The complex voicings of their identities in these three areas spoke not only backwards towards experi-ences in their pasts, but also forward to their hopes for themselves and the leaders who might follow in their steps.

Setting a Baseline: Case Studies | 3

Introduction

In undertaking to choose which interviews would be most appropriate to examine as case studies, it became readily apparent that two case studies of unlike natures would best provide a demonstration of the richness of the data present in all twenty-two of the transcripts. Therefore, the two women chosen as case studies were at opposite ends of the leadership spectrum, and provided an in-depth view of two quite dissimilar narratives of leadership development. Alice, twenty-eight, and at the beginning of her career, had been brought up in an environment that offered access to nearly every educational and social opportunity available to children in rural Northern Ireland. Alternatively, Doreen (twenty-four years Alice's senior, with decades of work experience) faced challenges that had kept her from participating in most of those same activities. In addition to their age and social differences, Alice's leadership development process had been shaped considerably by External Factors and Doreen's vastly more by Internal Factors.[11] The slight variations in data presentation between Alice and Doreen's case studies demonstrate the flexibility necessitated by incorporating such dissimilar voices, and the value of a methodology that creates space for such flexibility.

Exercising reflexivity throughout this study facilitated the identification of several roles I hold in relating socially and emotionally to the participant – those of academic, feminist and daughter of a rural family. Because these three roles are broad categories, each houses several positions from which I interacted with the participants. These positions are not without conflict, which required negotiating not only my relationship with the interviewee but internal relationships and dialogue with myself as well. These internal dialogues are incorporated into the case studies that follow as a means of clearly distinguishing between my voice and that of the participants.

3.1 Alice[12]

Introduction to the first case study

The analysis of this case study begins with the establishment of both the researcher and participant's social settings and the identification of the stories being told by the participant. This is followed by a discussion of the participant's self-descriptions, which were obtained by isolating her usage of the pronoun 'I' in the text. Next detailed are the voices from which this participant spoke in various portions of our discussion. The final portion describes the people, organizations and events that facilitated this participant's leadership journey.

3.1.1 Step 1 – Plot (Alice)

This initial step required listening for the plot being set forth by the interviewee – 'what is happening or what stories are being told' (Gilligan *et al.*, 2003) – as well as

noting my own reactions to her responses: where I connected with or disconnected from her story, our social locations and relationship to each other, and the
way that each of these might affect my interpretation of her story (Gilligan *et al.*,
2003). Within Alice's interview, I discovered three key stories relevant to her leadership development: Schooling process, Leadership journey and Involvement in
the Guiding Association.

Story number one: Schooling process

Alice and all of her siblings attended a local primary school and then transferred
to a larger school in a nearby town. Two reasons were given for this move: first, so
that they would have more opportunities to be involved in extracurricular activities; and secondly, to avoid an instructor who 'wasn't renowned for being a good
teacher'. Both reasons are reflective of Alice's affirmation that her family valued
education. She was elected a Prefect at her second school, which she described as
pushing the students to take advantage of more than just the 'educational things'.
When asked whether the school had differing expectations for male and female
students, she responded that they 'did everything together', including Home
Economics and Technology. In relating her schooling process, Alice was eager to
explain that she had relished her formal education, and mentioned in particular
the family feel of her second school:

> Um, and then I went through the [town] grammar school, which is, about-
> I think there's about six or seven hundred pupils; so it's reasonably small. It's
> really a nice family feel about it, I mean, everybody kind of knows everybody's
> from the local area. There's not that many people would travel, a- a- you know,
> we would probably be one of the furthest, about fifteen miles to go. So it's, kind
> of nice, size, nice family atmosphere and people to get involved in, in lots of
> things. Um. And the teachers all know, all the pupils and all the stu- I mean I,
> I really enjoyed my school, school education.

She described her family of origin as encouraging her and her siblings in
school without pushing them in a particular direction, and noted that she and all
of her siblings did their A-levels and went on to attend university. She did not 'rule
out' a graduate scheme, but took a job immediately after completing her university degree and had not pursued further education.

Story number two: Guiding Association involvement

Of the many and varied extracurricular activities that Alice participated in, her
experiences in the Guiding Association (or 'the Guides') seem to have shaped her
most. Throughout the interview, she returned to the Guides as a reference point
to explain and illustrate several different topics, most notably her perceptions of
the ways leadership should function. Having been involved with the Guides from
childhood until her marriage, she progressed through the association's leadership
training programme, receiving mentoring during the process:

> . . . I moved on through the Guides to become a Guide leader and did all of
> the qualifications for that so I suppose it- but it was an- a natural progression

for me more than anything, so. . . . I mean when you're, when we were doing our Guiding qualification, everyone's assigned a mentor to help them, just. But it's more to keep an eye on you, to make sure you're- 'Cause you have a, a book to fill in and tick off when you do y- mean there's loads of different wee things you have to do. Um, and reports you have to write, whatever, to get the- to get quali- qualified. So. The mentor is someone that checks that and helps you and guides you 'cause they've done it themselves.

It was within the framework of the Guides that Alice first gained experience at dividing leadership tasks according to strengths, sharing responsibility with a team:

And even within, I mean, our, our, the Guides I used to take, I was rubbish at, like craftwork. I was good at the sports. So, you know, we we were able to, you know, sort of, um align tasks according and, and then the people. So you have to, I mean leadership's only as good as the people around you.

Alice also directly attributed the attainment of her current occupational position to the inclusion on her CV of involvement in groups such as the Guides and the responsibility with which they had entrusted her:

Um, I mean I know I went for the job that I'm in now – Senior Policy Officer – when that came up there was two of us went for it in here, um, and th- what they told me was what made the difference was the kind of extra activities that I did outside work, including the leadership thing with the Guides and stuff. Because, you are given responsibilities there, taking, you know, ten girls away to camp, or whatever, and you obviously need to, have, sort of, those [laughs] skills to put up with them or whatever.

Story number three: Leadership journey

Alice's leadership journey was woven throughout her responses. Although most obviously labelled as 'leadership' in the training and experience she received through the Guiding Association, her involvement in other areas tells her leadership story just as clearly. When asked if she was seen as a natural leader as a child, she hesitantly admitted, 'Well, I suppose . . . yeah – to some extent'. Serving as the captain of a sports team, the Secretary of her chapter of Young Farmers, Sunday School and children's church leader, Prefect at secondary school and working with younger students in her summer job, Alice had many opportunities to exercise leadership before attaining the occupational position she held at the time of our interview. In that position, she was the chief advisor to a committee and gave presentations to large audiences, as well as having an 'area' that she 'look[ed] after' and was 'in charge of'.

Researcher's social location, relation to participant, emotional response

SOCIAL LOCATION: ACADEMIC   From the initial contact with Alice, throughout the interview and in the informal exchange at the end of the interview, it was my goal to put her at ease and convey that her level of education in no way defined the value of her words, opinions and experiences. Although I did not ask her if she

had intentions of pursuing further education, it is interesting to note in this context that she told me she had not 'ruled out' a graduate scheme even though she
had taken her current position because she qualified and it 'just . . . [came] up'.
It is possible that this was her means of asserting her equality with me in spite of
our differing levels of education, since it followed a description of her certainty
of what she did *not* want to do after university. However, it created a momentary
awkwardness on my part and I immediately sought to affirm her choice through
comparing her experience/choice with that of other women.

At times, I attempted to downplay my role as an academic and instead portray myself as a listener with whom she could feel comfortable. The interview
questions that required her to think specifically of her childhood or family experiences elicited some responses that indicated a lack of confidence in the relevance
of her answer to the study. In seeking to set her at ease, I was very quick to affirm
that her understanding of her childhood was correct and that obviously she would
not have been thinking in terms of this study while she was living through those
years.

SOCIAL LOCATION: FEMINIST   In assuring Alice of the appropriateness of her
responses, I was attempting to draw her out in ways that would not only make
her feel valued, but also elicit richer data for the study. This is a location that
I found significant although difficult to navigate, given the feminist mandate to
avoid exploiting research participants. In trying to balance the academic position
with the feminist, I relied heavily on the interview guide as a means of keeping
the conversation from veering far from the research questions and thus in some
way invalidating her input to the study by allowing our interaction to become so
conversational as to be irrelevant to the research topic.

During analysis, I noted several points at which I felt a strong negative reaction to Alice's responses because they initially appeared to support limitations
imposed on women by traditional gender roles. Her repeated insistence that there
was absolutely no difference between the treatment of male and female students
at her school was followed later in the interview by an adamant stance that her
current organization exhibited no discrimination, positive or negative, and treated
males and females the same, in spite of the fact that very few women served in
elected positions. This she described as 'nearly more of a practical thing rather
than, you know, a segregation'; but in continuing on attributed it to difficulties
with childcare provision and a recognition of the traditional role of rural women
in Northern Ireland as caregivers who stay home with the children. Alice also
asserted her position that although '. . . some would like to think that rural women
are, are hard done by or whatever . . . I don't feel that in *any* way'. After repeated
listenings, I was able to recognize this reaction on my part and to locate her
responses within the broader text, giving a fuller picture of her ideas regarding
women and gender roles.

Another concept that gave me pause was her use of the term 'merit' in speaking of how women advance in her organization. She described the organization
for which she worked as 'respect[ing] anyone on . . . their own merit', regardless of

gender. In particular, she cited her positive experience of giving presentations to groups of several hundred men, and the achievements of one woman who served as a committee chair while being very involved in working on the family farm and rearing five children. In order to value her voice, it was important for me to be able to put aside my assumptions regarding the role of merit in male-dominated organizations (e.g. Alston, 2003) and view her response as true in her experience.

SOCIAL LOCATION: DAUGHTER OF A RURAL FAMILY   It is from this position that I experienced the most connection with Alice. In conducting the listenings for analysis, I noted that throughout the beginning of the interview I repeatedly interjected brief stories of my life that seemed to be comparable to her childhood and educational experiences. I identified in this pattern my desire to be recognized and accepted by her as a rural woman despite my position as an academic and feminist. Because of the connection I felt with her and the similar experiences we shared as daughters of rural families, it was necessary to exercise particular care in analysing these aspects of her story so as to avoid replacing her voice with my own. Alternatively, there was much value in this connection, as it gave me the ability to understand her at points where a non-rural person might have been less informed.

3.1.2 Step 2 – I-Poems (Alice)

Derived from the use of the first-person 'I' in her interview transcript, Alice's (very lengthy) I-Poem produced a picture of her as a careful communicator who valued clarity in her speaking and the development of understanding in those who are listening. Through the use of the phrase 'I mean' she consistently elucidated her statements and asked, 'You know what I mean?' to be certain I was comprehending her meaning as well.

The I-Poem also revealed Alice's tendency to minimize her leadership experiences and abilities by using phrases that emphasized circumstances and other people rather than her own initiative. At times, she seemed almost surprised as she recognized her own leadership skills or experiences. For example, in speaking of her summer job working with younger children, she stated, '. . . that, I suppose, is very much a leadership role as well'. Consistent with this self-minimization was her commitment to the idea of leadership as a team effort, conveyed in phrases such as: 'I mean leadership's only as good as the people around you'; 'I don't think I'd like to be out on my own as a . . . leader'; and 'I mean . . . you need the strength of a good team around you'.

Finally, Alice's I-Poem showed the ability to form opinions and express her conviction in those opinions. This was especially clear in her assertions regarding gender roles in her family and at school: 'I was put out to do stuff in the garden as much as they were' (referring to her brothers); and 'I don't remember being *ever*, you know, any . . . differences' (between males and females at her school). However, these abilities were most obvious when she discussed the organization where she was employed: 'I mean . . . this organization, and, to be honest, this is my personal opinion, do not differentiate between men and women'; and 'I don't see any, like, discrimination at all or anything like that. I mean some people maybe do think that, but I really don't.'

3.1.3 Step 3 – Contrapuntal voices (Alice)

In the listenings of Steps 1 and 2, it initially appeared that Alice was uncertain or insecure about her responses; however, with further listening it became clear that, as noted above, her thoughtful way of speaking made her circumspect in responding to the interview questions. Building on the knowledge of her way of speaking which I attained during the first two steps, six distinct voices were identified for listenings in Step 3: Relational, Team Member, Leader, Uncertainty, Feminist and Traditionalist.

Each of these voices required a separate listening utilizing specific 'markers' to identify intervals at which Alice was speaking from that position (Gilligan *et al.*, 2003). Speaking positively regarding the value of relationships and their role in her life characterized the Relational voice. The Team Member voice affirmed and validated social groupings and organizations with which she was affiliated. Alice's Leader voice expressed strength of will, confidence, decisiveness and her ability to think critically about issues and maintain points of view she considered oppositional to the opinions of others. By minimizing the value of her leadership roles/experiences and occasionally vacillating on opinions that she expressed, Alice spoke in the voice of Uncertainty. The voice I have labelled 'Feminist' appeared in passages where Alice spoke of her determination to prove herself in situations involving men or in male-dominated settings; it was also apparent when she confidently affirmed her right to be in those situations/settings. Finally, Alice's articulation of experiences or ways of thinking that held true to traditional gender roles formed the Traditional voice.

Relational
Consistent with the findings of other research conducted with rural women (e.g. Walby, in Henig, 1996; Cunningham, 2008), Alice's emphasis on the importance of relationships originated with her family. She described her connection with her siblings as 'quite close in a way'. This was the first appearance of the Relational voice. Later in the interview, she again referenced her appreciation of family relationships when explaining, as noted above, that she appreciated her secondary school for its 'nice family atmosphere', and for the way students were known by teachers as well as other pupils.

The Relational voice clearly demonstrated her view of leadership as a relational activity throughout the interview. Although she portrayed herself as being part of a team of leaders in school, Alice's relational view of leadership was most notable in repeated references to the leadership training and experience she received through the Guiding Association. In this context, Alice spoke of sharing leadership responsibility with a team through assigning leadership tasks according to strengths. In addition, she repeatedly articulated the criteria she used to evaluate quality of leadership by remarks such as the following: 'I mean it's all about working – 'cause I mean at the end of the day, a leader is only as good as the team around you, so you want to be able to work well as a team'.

Team Member

This voice was most often characterized by a spirit of camaraderie and mutual assistance (or team efforts) in completing tasks, as well as demonstrating her loyalty to and appreciation of organizations and people with which she was associated. It appeared in the context of family at the beginning of her interview when she described the ways in which her entire family 'would have all helped out' on the farm, in her description of the encouragement her parents gave the children in terms of schooling, and her appreciation of her parents' sacrifice in facilitating their children's participation in extracurricular activities ('I'm glad that, you know, my parents did, cart us about the country and take us to all those organizations'). Her secondary school she described in glowing terms, including the ways in which the school had challenged her to achieve. The Team Member voice broached the subject of the Guiding Association many times in varied contexts including the value of such organizations to future job prospects.

Alice's Team Member voice was very nearly a protective voice. While showing her appreciation for the groups of people with which she identified, the Team Member voice occasionally took on a defensive tone. Referring to her parents' academic encouragement, Alice was quick to make the distinction that she and her siblings were not *pressured* by her parents in regard to their school performance (emphasis hers):

> I mean we were very much encouraged to do what we, wanted. Um, and to-
> you know we were encouraged in, in school very much so. And we were all, you
> know, we all did well in school. But we were never pushed in any particular
> direction. Um, it was very much- But I think we all had kind of ideas of where
> we want- We all wanted to go to university anyway, um without being *told* that,
> if you know what I mean. So, um, I don't know whether there was just an
> underlining expectation which we just kind of grew up with and followed or, or
> whether it was ourselves, but it just happened anyway. [laughs]

When asked about expectations her school may have held for males and females, her response again came in the Team Member voice (emphasis hers):

> Exactly the same. I don't remember being *ever* you know any, any, ever any
> differences. All our classes were mixed, you know. Home Economics, Technol-
> ogy, we did everything together. So there was no difference made between
> males/females.

The Team Member voice appeared especially defensive when asked whether her organization provided support for women who aspired to leadership:

I mean, uh, this organization, and to be honest, this is my personal opinion, do not differentiate between men and women . . . I mean- it's- there's no, there's just no mention of male/female. I mean, it's just- there's no discrimination or positive discrimination, you know for or against . . .

She later revisited the point, stating (emphasis hers):

I mean, this organization is by *far*, um, a male-dominated organization, but, they respect anyone on the merit, you know, on their own merit. I mean, I, I've never felt, you know, that they've looked down on me in any way because I'm a woman. . . . I don't think there's- I don't think th- I don't see, any, like, discrimination at all or anything like that. I mean, some people maybe do think that, but I really don't.

In every response regarding her family, schooling, and work organization, Alice presented a positive description and cited examples of positive actions on their parts.

Leader

From descriptions of her childhood actions and thought processes through to her current position, Alice (many times unselfconsciously) spoke in the voice of a Leader. In this voice, she showed pride in her educational accomplishments, and described herself as desiring to succeed on her own merit. As a child, she had demonstrated determination to succeed (such as attempting activities that required greater physical strength than she felt she possessed). Regarding school, she showed initiative by desiring a university education 'without being *told*' that she needed to further her education. In the context of our interview, she showed self-confidence when – without being prompted – she corrected responses that I inaccurately summarized or misunderstood. Her self-confidence also showed in her expression of opinions that she recognized could possibly be controversial or in disagreement with my views, as at the end of the interview, when asked if there was anything more she would like to add (emphasis hers):

I don't, I don't think so. I mean. I don't think, um. I mean. I think there would be some, some would like to think that rural women are, are hard done by or whatever and I don't feel that in *any* way.

When speaking directly of her leadership experiences, Alice expressed her enjoyment of those activities, and at points validated her leadership abilities:

I mean I did work as well, maybe didn't mention this, as a, during the summer I'd helped with, well, I got paid to work in the summer scheme in [town]. Each of the Councils in Northern Ireland would run summer schemes which are just programmes during the summer for kids, what about, age, say, five to sixteen. Depends on the area. And you take them off to different places and all the rest of it and, play games with them. And, and that, I suppose, is very much a leadership role as well.

Additionally, her Leader voice advocated practical leadership experience as a means of attaining occupational goals:

But. You can't get there unless you have experience at a, a, younger- younger age. Um, I mean there are opportunities I suppose to – you can learn all the leadership stuff you want in books and courses, but I think that you need a bit of practical experience at the end of the day.

Uncertainty

Although confident in many ways, Alice also consistently demonstrated ambiguity regarding her status as a leader. Most frequently this took the form of expressing doubt regarding two factors: the legitimacy of the label 'leader' as it applied to her experiences, and the source of her motivation to achieve. The Uncertainty voice was often cloaked in phrases such as 'it just happened', or 'I suppose'. Her account of obtaining the post she occupied at the time of our interview illustrates the Uncertainty voice, even as she asserted her confidence that she knew what she *didn't* want to do (emphasis hers):[13]

> L: *Did you try to get in like an entry-level position with an organization or did you want something that was a little more responsibility?*
>
> A: I mean, it was just, I mean whenever I qualified this job came up, applied for it and I got it and that was that, but you know within the [organization] people do tend to come in as graduates. Not always. But do tend to come in as graduates, or, or maybe as sort of, first or second, you know, job- a-after a couple of years working somewhere else they come in here. So you tend to have starting quite young. Sooo, I suppose it's sort of an entry, you know . . .
>
> L: *Right.*
>
> A: . . . but. It's not – I mean, we've another girl who's worked elsewhere for maybe twenty years and has started in the same position as I started in.
>
> L: *So it's an . . .*
>
> A: But at that stage, you know, when you just qualify, you just, like, 'Oh, whatever' you know, 'comes up'.
>
> L: *Yeah. [laughs]*
>
> A: It wasn't. I mean I didn't – I knew what I *didn't* want to do, and I didn't want to go into Price Waterhouse Coopers and do an accountancy degree and a graduate scheme like that. Or accountancy scheme or a graduate scheme. So. But I didn't rule out, a graduate scheme with someth-, you know, in some other organization. So I just, it's just the way it happened more than my choice, you know.

Even when recounting activities in which she had clearly exercised leadership (e.g. captain of a sports team, teacher of a class, leader in the Guides) she attempted to negate the title 'leader' through simplification of the situation and minimization of the importance of her role. Regarding her time as a leader in her school, she remarked:

> A: A lot of it was, rather than picking out an individual it was elected, amongst the other pupils as much as anything else. So it depended. I mean

> I didn't, apart from being a Prefect which was an elected, I didn't have any
> specific leadership role in school, um apart from being one of a team of leaders
> if you know what I mean. [smiles]

Interestingly, the voice of Uncertainty was at times present in statements that expressed a strong opinion. It showed itself in verbal stops and starts within the statement, as if Alice was attempting to de-emphasize the statement to avoid controversy or giving offence (as can be seen in her comments above regarding rural women not being 'hard done by'). At various points, as she thought more deeply about her experiences, it appeared that Alice recognized for the first time the leadership qualities which she had demonstrated in some of her experiences. The statements in which the Uncertainty voice can be heard did not always contain stops and starts, but occasionally took on a confessional tone, as when she stated (with a smile):

> I find the word leader a bit strange, 'cause I don't see myself as a leader
> 'cause I always rely on, you know, other people around me and all the things,
> you know. I don't think I'd like to be out on my own as a, as a, a leader, you
> know.

Feminist

The term 'feminist' in this context can only be said to relate to indirect statements by Alice, who at no point verbally labels herself 'feminist'. However, many of her stories were told in a voice that spoke in agreement with feminist ideals, and therefore were labelled the 'Feminist' voice. Her stories of early years with her family were especially formative of the Feminist voice, wherein she showed her evaluation of herself as equal to her male siblings in their work on their family's farm. Alice's Feminist voice also spoke when she recounted helping at her father's business, saying she was 'probably not able to do as much of the physical work, but would have had a good . . . attempt at it'.

Concerning education, the Feminist voice spoke of being encouraged to pursue educational goals of her choosing, and also of traditionally gender-segregated courses which males and females participated in together. When asked for advice she might give to young women like herself, Alice directed her response regarding schooling to both 'boys **and** girls' (emphasis hers). This view of the applicability of situations to both males and females carried over into her descriptions of the 'male-dominated' organization where she worked, as well. Her repeated emphasis on the lack of 'discrimination or positive discrimination' at her workplace provided the context for her assertion that she would prefer to achieve based on merit rather than gender: 'I mean you'd rather just get there on your own merits rather than because you're a girl'.

Desiring gender-neutral working contexts influenced the Feminist voice's expression of ideas regarding leadership, as well. In emphasizing the importance of having a support team for leadership, Alice stated that gender was not a factor in the makeup of the team:

So if you're going into an organization, if there're others all with the same kind of enthusiasm for whatever, whether it's a sport, whether it's with working with young children, or whether it's maybe conservation or something activities, or whatever. If you've got a good team of people with you all- you know, that are helping you, um. I think that's the support network that you, you need. Um. A- and I don't think, matters whether they're male or female either.

Further in the interview, she described achieving respect as a leader regardless of the gender makeup of the group being led. The final story in her interview further illustrated her belief in gender-neutral achievement as she spoke admiringly of a woman who functioned as the chair of a committee within Alice's organization:

A: [O]ne of our Chairmen is a lady called [name] who's, you know, chairs our [committee], which is – an important committee within, within the [organization]. Um, she's also a mum. I think she's five kids, um . . .

L: *Oh my goodness.*

A: Uh, she's a farmer's wife. She, she sits on, she does a lot around the h- the home place. And she's involved- She works. I mean she's just- She's a- she's really . . .

L: *She does everything! [laughs]*

A: . . . a neat person. She does everything. Um, and I know [she] would, I mean, again, have got to where she is on her own merit, not because of her sex, you know.

L: *Yeah.*

A: It's just because she's, she's great, you know, at what she does. And, and the chair, the committee that she chair- chairs in the [organization] is, is an important one. And she has just a, a fantastic understanding of- it's all about the funding programmes, you know, for agriculture. And she's just a great understanding and that's why she got the job, because she was, you know, so, so, well, um, informed on the whole issue, so.

Traditional

Alice's description of her upbringing as 'traditional' formed the foundation of her Traditional voice. Quite early in the interview she gave two illustrations of her idea of traditional experiences. In the first, she described the area where she was reared:

So it was, bu- I mean, a- remote in that sense that when you're younger you can't get anywhere unless someone takes you or whatever. Umm. Yep! So grew up with, on- in our house, but it was surrounded by my uncle's farm. Um, so and a lot of fa- other family nearby. Traditional.

In the second illustration, she demonstrated the traditional role she held within the house in regard to chores, but went on to clarify her awareness of the traditional tone of her description:

L: And did you have specific jobs around the house that were yours, or chores that were yours that you always had to do or . . .

A: Not specifically. I mean we all held out – we all helped out in different areas. I suppose the boys tended to do the, stuff outside and whatever, um and I helped mom inside, you know, like you know and whatever. But. I mean I was put out to do the stuff in the garden as much as they were.

Some of the leadership roles she held before university also fell within gender roles that could be considered traditional, as they involved caring for younger children. Her description of a Prefect's duties, in particular, showed traditional gender role ideation in its usage of the terms 'look after', 'help' and 'role model':

And Prefects in a sense were, a, kind of leadership role. And when we were- w-
If you were a Senior Prefect, you were all given a junior class to look after, and
help the teacher and be like a role model for those. So I mean, I was a Prefect
at school.

The Traditional voice was quite strong when Alice spoke regarding the involvement of women in her current organization. Insistent that the organization did not discriminate against women, she instead attributed women's lack of involvement to tradition, saying, '. . . somebody has to stay at home and look after the kids', and noting that historically this has been women's role. Finally, her admiration for the woman who chaired a committee in Alice's organization, worked on the family farm, and was mother to five children clearly demonstrated Alice's ability to appreciate traditional gender roles.

Synthesis of voices

The contrapuntal voices present in Alice's responses related to each other in various ways. At times they were in agreement. At other times they contradicted each other. Most often they appeared singly in long strands of dialogue, only to be followed by another long strand of dialogue in a different voice. The transition from voice to voice was seamless in nearly every instance – the voice of Uncertainty being the most notable shift, with its verbal stops and starts.

The voices that were most often in agreement with each other were the Feminist voice and the Team Member voice. This seems surprising, given the independence expressed by the Feminist voice. However, upon closer inspection, this harmony of voices demonstrated Alice's appreciation for people and organizations that affirmed her idea of herself and other women as persons who have the right to attempt and achieve, regardless of gender. Unsurprisingly, the Feminist voice and the Leader voice also spoke agreeably in several places, showing that her determination and strength of will frequently carried over into her opinions regarding gender roles.

Two particular combinations demonstrated opposition between voices, the first being the interweaving of Uncertainty with Relational and Team Member. The Uncertainty voice, which was at odds with her more confident voices, spoke frequently. Although deeply committed to the positive value of relationships in any leadership context, Alice utilized the Uncertainty voice in conjunction with the Relational and Team Member voices in a negative way to minimize (or nullify) her individual importance as a leader.

A second oppositional combination of voices can be found in the Feminist voice and the Traditionalist voice. While speaking in her Feminist voice, Alice continually affirmed the valuing of women by her organization and asserted that the organization 'Would love more . . . women to get involved'. However, the Traditional voice immediately followed by saying '. . . it's nearly more a practical thing rather than, you know, a segregation, because somebody has to stay at home and look after the kids . . .', thereby implying that this was a woman's role. Thus she, perhaps unknowingly, illustrated lack of childcare as a barrier to involvement – one that is common for many rural women in Northern Ireland (Rural Women's Networks, Northern Ireland Rural Women's Network, 2007). This was compounded at the end of the interview by her admiring description of the mother of five who also serves as committee chair and farmhand. This placed childcare again firmly in the realm of traditional gender roles, making it women's primary concern – one that must be observed in addition to or at the expense of other commitments (Bock and de Haan, 2004).

3.1.4 Analysis (Alice)

The research questions served as the framework for analysing Alice's interview. Analysis began with the ways in which specific people, organizations and events contributed to her leadership development. Following this, it turned to an examination of the role of Alice's individual thought processes and choices in both the supportive and non-supportive contexts she faced in her leadership development.

External factors: People, organizations and events
Each of Alice's voices came together to tell multi-faceted stories of specific people, organizations and events that shaped her leadership development. From the subjectivity of personal perceptions to the relative objectivity of organizational procedures and processes, a great deal of information regarding the formative contributions of these factors was present in her narrative. Each category will be discussed in detail below, incorporating both the subjective and (relatively) objective experiences that she recounted.

External Factors: People
FAMILY   Alice's leadership journey began with her family of origin, in which she was the eldest child. To them can be attributed an important portion of her view of herself as having the right to attempt – and being capable of attempting – tasks that traditionally have been assigned to or performed by males. By sharing tasks and attempting tasks with her male siblings, Alice developed the basis for confidence and comfort in her current involvement as a leader in a male-dominated organization.

Family also played a valuable role in facilitating Alice's educational successes. Although admitting that she was uncertain whether her and her siblings' completion of A-levels and university was the result of personal choice or 'under-lying expectation', Alice described her family as very encouraging in terms of educational achievement. Equally importantly, she portrayed her parents' encour-agement as positive rather than pressuring or controlling.

Her family's involvement in organizations led to Alice's involvement in orga-nizations as well. Alice described her mother and father and both of their families as being 'involved in lots of organizations', including church activities, but admit-ted that as a child she had not considered the influence of observing this involve-ment on her own leadership development. Her parents enabled Alice to participate in organizations such as the Guides, and encouraged her to take on the responsi-bility of teaching children in their church. Additionally, Alice expressed gratitude to her parents for 'cart[ing]' her and her siblings 'about the country' to sport, dance and music activities.

OTHER SIGNIFICANT PEOPLE   Outside her family, Alice mentioned a handful of specific people who were influential in her leadership development. Education-ally, the pupils and teachers at her secondary school provided a familial envi-ronment that she appreciated and in which she thrived. They also afforded her leadership experience by electing her as Prefect. The only experience she rec-ognized as mentoring came through the Guiding Association, which provided a mentor for her as she trained to be a leader in their organization. However, she also spoke highly of a woman in her current organization, and seemed to admire her management of work, family and farm responsibilities. Finally, the Chief Executive at her organization had confirmed her relational view of leadership in saying that their strength as an organization lay with 'the team of people we have, not any one individual'.

External Factors: Organizations

SCHOOL   Organizations figured prominently in Alice's growth as a leader. The second school she attended – described by her as 'reasonably small', with 600 to 700 pupils – encouraged both male and female students to participate in extra-curricular activities and to take courses in a variety of subject areas. In so doing, it fostered in her a sense that there was no difference in the school's expectations for males and females. Her leadership experience in the school took place in the shape of a team of leaders, and was a positive one.

COMMUNITY-BASED ORGANIZATIONS   Through her schooling years, she was involved in several community-based organizations, and when asked if she had been a natural leader as a child, these provided a context from which she was able to answer affirmatively. The Guiding Association, in particular, not only shaped her view of leadership as a team function, but also provided a 'natural progres-sion' for her to complete a leadership qualification, which she noted as her only formal leadership training and described as emphasizing team building. In addi-tion to the Guiding Association, Alice also enjoyed teaching both Sunday School and Children's Church and serving as Secretary in a local rural young people's organization. Such involvement in community institutions was high on her list of recommendations for young rural people, both male and female, who wish to become leaders.

CURRENT EMPLOYER   Alice's leadership skills and ideas were continuing to be formed by her current occupational position. Having qualified for the post imme- diately after university, it was her first position of leadership outside school and community organizations, and she was putting into practice her previously gained principles of leadership. Though she held fast to the ideal of relational or team leadership, Alice described her position as mostly independent work, preceded and followed by periods of consultation with the committee that she advised. That committee frequently asked for her recommendations on policies in her area of expertise, and she assuredly described herself as having opportunities to influ- ence policy and give her opinion. Building on experiences in mixed male/female settings, she had confidently made presentations to large groups of men, and felt that she was received without discrimination. In addition, she characterized the organization as supporting training and advancement on the basis of merit rather than gender, which fit with her desire to achieve based on her own merit rather than policies of positive discrimination.

EVENTS   One of the most influential events on Alice's leadership development was the changing of schools when she was a child. By leaving the smaller rural school and travelling to a larger town school, she gained access to a much broader spectrum of activities and opportunities. In addition to a simple change in loca- tion, however, this school also required her to complete her General Certificate of Secondary Education (exam-based, subject-specific awards commonly referred to as GCSEs), which was a significant achievement. As stated above, this change of schools eventually led to her election as Prefect, giving her the opportunity to exercise leadership among her peers – another valuable event in her leadership journey. A second notable happening was only mentioned by Alice in passing – her marriage. It was this event that ended her involvement as a leader in the Guides, which she contextualized as having been a meaningful part of her life for many years. Finally, being hired into her current job was quite an important event in Alice's life, giving her the opportunity to put into practice the skills she had honed to that point and to continue in her evolution as a leader.

Internal factors: Individual thought processes and choices

Throughout the interview, Alice articulated several underlying assumptions. The most prominent of these was the seemingly unconscious masking of personal choices as natural progression in her descriptions of situations and experiences. Many expressions of this theme included the word 'just': 'it just happened', 'it was just . . .', 'you just . . .'. When this line of thinking regarded her own life, she dem- onstrated an expectation that things would progress for her along a particular path. For example, in describing her continuance to university education from secondary school, she was uncertain as to why she made the choice, but laughed when she stated, 'it just happened anyway'. This attitude followed her through university and became the lens through which she interpreted her choice to work for the organization by which she was currently employed: '. . . I just, it's just the way it happened more than my choice, you know'. These assumptions are a clear reflection of her family's social position, given the fact that her participation in many of the educational and extracurricular activities was made possible by her parents' ability to provide a means of accessing those opportunities. However, for Alice, they were simply a matter of fact. This viewpoint had served her well by facilitating her attainment of a university degree and a leadership position within her organization.

Alice's articulation of her own leadership experiences demonstrated the assumption that what she had accomplished was nothing extraordinary, but instead simply the product of circumstance. Crediting her childhood exercise of leadership abilities to organizational involvement, she described becoming a leader in the Guides as a 'natural progression' for her because of the organization's structure. Alice also attributed her successful application for the post she currently held to participation in community organizations/activities and sports rather than any particular personal qualities.

Not all of Alice's thought processes minimized her abilities and choices, however. From her childhood attitude of equality with her brothers came her adult desire to succeed based on merit, which she had parlayed into a position of leadership in a male-dominated organization. Her experience in leading children she translated into leadership competencies useful with adults as well, laughingly saying the 'same skills will work with both'. Showing initiative throughout her youth and in her (somewhat unconscious) decision to continue to university, Alice was aware of what she did *not* want in a career, and accepted an occupational post that allowed her to continue to operate as a self-motivated and independent worker/thinker. Building on the example of cooperation her family provided, the teamwork and team-building of the Guides, and serving on a team of leaders in school, Alice fashioned a concept of leadership based on willingness to accept any supportive and helpful person as part of her leadership team – an attitude that greatly aided her in her position as an advisor to a committee and in her work as part of a team. Alice expressed enjoyment of her practical experiences of leadership and confidence in being identified as a rural woman.

3.2 Doreen[14]

Introduction to the second case study

The selection of this narrative for treatment as a case study was based upon two strategic factors. First, the speaker's role as a rural woman in leadership is an excellent representation of many of the participants' leadership experiences. Secondly, the respondent was a woman who overcame numerous personal difficulties on the path to leadership: poverty, an alcoholic parent, early cessation of education, harassment for being the child of a mixed (Catholic/Protestant) marriage, and the economic and personal stresses of starting a business only to face economic recession and the loss of her secondary job. Her circumstances – while extreme in comparison with most other participants' – are not entirely unique in this study. Nor are they unique among rural women in Northern Ireland. For these reasons, this woman's voice is of particular interest in the attempt to discover factors that facilitate leadership development among women from a variety of social backgrounds.

Doreen was fifty-two years old at the time of our interview. She held a management post at a rural women's centre, which involved teaching personal development courses and coordinating funding for the centre, among other duties. She had been married for thirty-five years and was the mother of five children. In addition to her full-time job at the centre, she travelled (in her words) 'all over Ireland' with her husband, and also coordinated a programme for women at her church, where she served on the Board of Directors and was regarded as a Pastor.

3.2.1 Step 1 – Plot (Doreen)

As with the first case study, this step required listening for stories being told by the interviewee as well as noting my connections to, and disconnections from, her responses. This segment details our social locations and relationship to each other, and the ways that each of these had the potential to affect my interpretation of her story (Gilligan *et al.*, 2003). Doreen's interview revealed five key stories relevant to the research question: Childhood poverty, Schooling process, Leadership journey, Spirituality and Helping other women.

Researcher's social location, relation to participant and emotional response
EMOTIONAL RESPONSE   In the first case study, my emotional responses to the participant were included in the descriptions of the social locations that she and I inhabited. However, Doreen's interview drew particularly strong emotional reactions from me, and these must be addressed at the outset of the analysis in order to achieve the disclosure necessary to distinguish between her voice and that of the researcher. Listening to her responses in the actual interview setting was tremendously rewarding, if difficult in places. However, the reading, re-reading, listening and re-listening done during analysis proved surprisingly emotionally arduous. Her deeply personal stories allowed a connection with her on a very basic, human level, and her relative comfort in recounting her experiences (which she did quite frequently in various social settings) facilitated these feelings of connection to her as an individual. This affinity was not based on the similarities of our life stories, but rather on the differences between them and on the compassion I felt for her younger self as the child of a poor family and an alcoholic parent. Interestingly, many of her stories – especially those from her childhood – were also places of disconnection for me as I viewed them from a social position that seemed relatively privileged in comparison. At points I was emotionally connected to her and simultaneously socially disconnected from her 'otherness'.

It is important to make a distinction here between my feelings of compassion for Doreen, and pity – which could have become the focal lens through which I analysed her interview. Doreen's indomitable spirit became that lens instead. It is in that statement that I disclose one of the most difficult points of analysing her interview: frank admiration for this woman's achievements and her ability to overcome adversity presented a challenge to maintaining a balanced perspective on the information contained in her interview. However, that admiration also provided a starting point in the search for 'positive' factors in Doreen's leadership journey.

SOCIAL LOCATION: ACADEMIC   As may be inferred from the preceding paragraphs, Doreen's interview was one in which I found it difficult to maintain an 'objective' academic position. However, because of Doreen's own personality and educational accomplishments, at no point did she appear to be intimidated by my advanced education or the fact that she was participating in an academic study. Rather, my position as an academic allowed me to share in the triumph she expressed when describing her return to education as a thirty-five-year-old farmer's wife, partner in a failing business, and mother of five.

SOCIAL LOCATION: FEMINIST   As a feminist researcher, I was interested in expressions of traditional experiences of gender roles and attitudes in Doreen's transcript. In several instances, I was fascinated to discover that she had taken what appeared to be a traditional role or experience and moulded it to suit her personality and/or goals. While her narrative is replete with stories of family members who acted according to traditional roles, she repeatedly took leaps outside those confines. From a feminist perspective, those non-traditional places inhabited by Doreen provided me with a personal connection to her, as I admired the courage she showed in breaking with family and cultural norms. Additionally, they created a point from which to view her as valuing feminist ideals, although she did not verbally identify herself as such.

Relatively early in the interview, Doreen informed me that she had obtained a diploma in Women's Studies. Further, her work centred on helping women in difficult circumstances become confident enough to take steps to change their lives. Because of this, I found that I was less anxious about being perceived personally as a feminist – and about the obviously feminist nature of my research – than I had been in other interviews where participants expressed dislike for the feminist movement or the label 'feminist'.

SOCIAL LOCATION: PARTICIPANT IN THE CHRISTIAN TRADITION   This topic is a deeply personal one and not an area I had anticipated including in this work – both because it in some ways exposes my personal beliefs to academic scrutiny, and because I wish to distance myself from the possibility of being connected in any way to the many negative stereotypes associated with Christianity. However, the integral role of religious faith in this interview makes it a necessary topic of discussion here.

Doreen's childhood Sundays were spent travelling three miles on foot each way to attend services and Sunday School at several different churches. It was not surprising to me, then, when later in the interview she rather tentatively told me that she was involved in her local congregation and also travelled and spoke with her husband in religious settings. Having had a similar experience in my own life, I was eager to make that connection with her. She was delighted, but still seemed uncertain as to how appropriate a discussion of her faith might be in relation to the study. During the actual interview, when Doreen excitedly whispered, 'I just love Jesus', it gave me a glimpse at her deep passion for her faith and its role in shaping her life. However, in listening back to the interview and reading through the transcript, I observed that my eagerness to connect on this topic became momentary discomfort and concern as I recognized that freely sharing that portion of my life might possibly have given her an incorrect picture of the type of faith I had or the depth of similarity between our stories, thus building a sense of trust and safety that could easily be perceived afterwards as exploitative. I was also concerned with the possibility that the discussion of Doreen's faith might be of a more fundamentalist or charismatic nature than I would be able to contain and focus as an interviewer.

While I recognize that for many researchers this may not have presented a problem, my experiences as a life-long participant in Christian churches have exposed me to facets of that faith that seemed to have no place in the setting of an academic study interview. Because of this concern, I was relieved to hear her speak of the boundaries she adhered to between the faith-based seminars she led at her church and the seminars that she gave at the centre. As Doreen continued to express her passion for God and Jesus, it became imminently apparent that her faith took the form of loving service for others, and that she used it as a means of building confidence and self-appreciation among the women she served rather than as an exclusionary measure. The end result of our inclusion of the subject of faith was a much richer conversation – one that allowed Doreen to truly communicate her deepest sense of self and identity.

Story number one: Childhood poverty

Doreen's portrayal of her childhood home centred on the poverty of her family of origin. Describing her father's alcoholism as contributing to their status as 'impoverished' and 'disadvantaged', she nevertheless viewed her childhood as 'quite happy'. One of the most memorable aspects of Doreen's childhood narrative was her description of walking three miles each way to and from school, particularly unpleasant in seasons of cold weather. Although her father's extended family lived nearby, and helped the family with donations of food when possible, Doreen's mother's family was estranged from Doreen's immediate family. The event with the most far-reaching consequences for Doreen was the expectation that – because of her family's financial difficulties and in spite of the educational potential her teachers saw in her – she would leave school at a young age in order to seek work and contribute to the family's income.

Story number two: Schooling process
Doreen's schooling process provided a unique and positive narrative. After leaving school at age fifteen, she married into a wealthy family (at seventeen) and in succeeding years had five children. Twenty years after exiting the educational system, she rekindled her love of learning by taking a course at a local university. With her husband's encouragement, and showing great determination as she also gave full-time care to five children, she completed not only the original course, but also a follow-up course and, eventually, a diploma.

Story number three: Leadership journey
In choosing to take a different path from that of most of the women in her family (who stayed home or worked in factories) Doreen showed the potential for leadership. Unable to pursue nursing, which had been her childhood dream, she became a nursing auxiliary after her marriage. Later, she set up a business with her husband. After an economic downturn caused the business to collapse, Doreen returned to school. Exercising her capabilities as a visionary, she set and surpassed the goal of earning £15 per hour within three years of her attendance in that first course. After completing her diploma, she was hired as facilitator for a programme at the university, and eventually took up what she considered her first leadership position as Chairperson of her local women's group. Following on from that position, she held a variety of leadership positions with several rural organizations, travelled as a speaker, and served as a pastor and member of the board of directors in her local congregation.

Story number four: Spirituality
As the child of a Catholic/Protestant mixed marriage, Doreen described her father as 'always trying to prove that, um, that we were brou- were being brought up as Protestants'. Thus, she and her siblings spent their Sundays travelling from church to church attending a variety of Sunday Schools and services. The work in which she was involved at the women's centre and at her church stemmed from a deep faith in and love for God – whom she smilingly referred to at one point as 'my Dad'. She facilitated cross-community events for women with the goal of breaking through the 'barriers' and 'religious stuff' they had learned through the years. Her ultimate goal was to be a full-time pastor.

Story number five: Helping other women
The experiences of Doreen's childhood fuelled her desire to help other women who found themselves in similar circumstances. From her posts in the women's centre and at her church, she was able to reach out to many such women for whom she had 'so much compassion'. As a means of building their faith and self-confidence, she held personal development courses in both locations – focusing on 'assertiveness, confidence building and the power of positive thinking' at the women's centre, and on the setting and achievement of goals at the church. Her fight for funding for the women's centre was also a product of her desire to

continue to provide support for women, some of whom she said, 'would not be here, today' if not for the centre.

3.2.2 Step 2 – I-Poem (Doreen)

Doreen's I-Poem reveals a beautifully constructed outline of her story and the view she had of herself and the women she worked with. A few key phrases reveal her internal voice with great clarity: 'I mean', 'I remember' and 'I look' (or 'I see'). These phrases intertwine throughout the interview multiple times in various contexts, facilitating a vibrant understanding of Doreen's self-concept as conveyed by her first-person voice. Additionally, Doreen's voice changed from passive to active as she transitioned from childhood and poverty into adulthood and wealth in the home of her husband's family.

'I mean'

At the beginning of her interview, the phrase 'I mean' revealed at Doreen's core a deep awareness of the challenges she faced in her family of origin. It also demonstrated a cultivated mindfulness that allowed her to draw out the differences between what the listener might have been conceptualizing and the realities of the story she was telling. For example, when asked about jobs or chores she had in her childhood home, she used 'I mean' to juxtapose the family's poverty over what could be considered a relatively benign or typical domestic scene and bring the listener back to the realities Doreen's family faced (emphasis mine):

> L: *Did you have particular chores or jobs that were yours to do around the house, or . . .?*

> D: Yeah. Very much so, because we were- you know, there was seven of us, very much so. So, there was an expectation, particularly on the Saturday morning, that you, you know, that the girls did their own bedroom. And, there was an expectation to do the ironing, and also then to help with weeding, weeding the garden and, and things like that so there was. Yeah. Very much so. And also then, we also had to walk, you know, there was three miles- we lived from three miles from the village. So we had to always walk to the village, for our groceries, and . . .

> L: *On a Saturday?*

> D: Yeah. Yeah. So we always walked. Well sometimes my mom would have come in after school and would have met us after school. So it ended up that, she probably had a baby in the pram, and then, loads of groceries at the bottom of the pram [slightly laughing], underneath the pram, and, and all of that, you know. But **I mean**, you had to walk. You had to virtually walk for, for everything.

> L: *Did you walk that far to school as well?*

> D: Yeah, yeah, uh huh. And that – well, that wasn't very nice in the winter time.

Throughout the course of our conversation, Doreen's usage of 'I mean' continued to serve as a precursor to stories of herself and others in what she appeared to consider atypical circumstances. As a leader, she used 'I mean' to relate stories that demonstrated her concern for women in her centre who were experiencing particular personal difficulties (emphasis mine):

> **I mean**, even when they didn't turn up I would have jumped in the car and went and encouraged them to come in. **I mean**. And some of them the stories are- They're just wee, oh . . . They're just wee darlings. I just love them to bits. . . . I just know, Lori, that some of them wouldn't be here today. You know, [starts to cry] they would be- committed suicide or what – you know what **I mean**?

Doreen's utilization of the phrase 'I mean' usually preceded a statement supporting her point or, more commonly, a substantiating illustration from her own life. 'I mean' became an expression of her self-concept, assisting her in creating a space where the listener could, without feeling hopeless, fully engage with the painful situations she described. In this way, 'I mean' encapsulates Doreen's interpretation of her own story and that of the women she leads – a difficult one, but not without hope.

'I remember'

'I remember' was a powerful statement for Doreen. It appeared throughout the interview – most frequently in the first half, as she discussed her childhood – and seemed to represent more than a straightforward recollection of facts. When Doreen spoke the words 'I remember', it was as if she was vividly reliving the moments she described, rather than simply experiencing the emotions – both positive and negative – associated with the stories in her narrative. Interestingly, Doreen's I-Poem reveals that 'I remember' precedes stories describing key moments of awareness or change in her life, such as being teased by other children because of her parents' mixed marriage. She also utilized 'I remember' when recounting the difference between living in poverty at home with her family of origin and moving into the home of her husband's wealthy family after marriage.

A further example of the power of this phrase in her narrative can be found in the retelling of a crucial moment in Doreen's leadership journey. She began with 'I remember' and brought the intensity of her job loss and the choice to return to education into the present through her words and inflections (emphasis in bold mine):

> So it ended up, we were paid off, and **I remember** this big sign out at the back of . . . Women's Group, and it said, 'January Starting Course in the University of Ulster: Time for Me'. And I thought: 'Time for Me'. And I, I thought about it, you know, at home that night, and I thought about it, Lori, and I thought, 'This *is* time for me'. You know, this- 'I can actually take that step that I've always wanted to take, and it is now time for me'.

In making use of 'I remember' as a bridge for acutely bringing the reality of the past into present conversations, Doreen revealed both her ability to synthesize the experiences of her life into tools of change for others and her desire to do so. As with Doreen's usage of 'I mean', 'I remember' showed that her need to express the depth of her experiences and thought processes went beyond a self-serving retelling and instead communicated a more social understanding of the purpose behind her story.

'I look' (or 'I see')
The concept of seeing and being seen seemed to be of great importance to Doreen. The phrase 'I was seen' was used only one time in the narrative of her childhood (emphasis mine):

> Um, well I was the second, I was the second child and I suppose I would have been regarded as the one, as being more brainier than any of the rest of them, you know. **I was seen** as the one that would have had more skills . . .

Obviously this description of herself is a positive one, and therefore the limitation of its usage to one time in the stories of her childhood led me to consider the possibility that she felt *un*seen much of the time within her family of origin.

This was also brought to mind when she spoke later in the interview regarding the women with whom she worked at the centre. However, consistent with her usage of 'I mean' and 'I remember', Doreen used her positivity[15] once again to transform that lack of being seen into the ability to 'see' herself and a determination to 'see' the women she helped in her capacity as leader. The I-Poem reflects her journey of seeing and being seen in a manner that clearly illustrates this:

Childhood (birth to age 17)
I was seen
When I look back on it
I look back on it
I look back on it
I can't really see

Adulthood
I see myself
When I look back on it
When I look back on it
I see so many people
I look at them
I look at some of those women
I look at them
I look at them
I look at her
I just look

The I-Poem also powerfully demonstrates the internal shift that accompanied changes in Doreen's social position. The transition that took place at the time of her marriage opened the potential for her to inhabit a position in which she could observe and interact with her life differently from how she had as a child. Thus, she moved internally from a place of invisibility ('I can't really see') to a place of vision ('I see myself'). Doreen then used this movement from invisibility to self-awareness as a template for assisting women in her centre, by first seeing them and then helping them to see themselves.

Passive voice to active voice

For much of the childhood portion of her interview, Doreen spoke in a passive voice that seemed to convey the idea that things were happening around her or to her, but were not necessarily her choice. For example:

> 'I never had the opportunity [to attend grammar school]', and

> 'I wanted to become a nurse . . . I *didn't* become a nurse.'

At the time of her return to education at thirty-five, however, Doreen's voice changed from passive to active, as she began to take courses and pursue objectives she had not previously considered attainable. In the active voice, she recounted her determination to complete her coursework even when she felt like dropping out because of the level of stress she experienced: 'I did it', 'I *went* for it' and 'I kept in there'.

The active voice not only expressed Doreen's internal evolution, but also an outward turning in her community involvement as well as she spoke about becoming involved in leadership at the women's centre and in her church. Her desire to help the women around her came from a continual revisiting of the events of *her* past in order to help them understand and gain perspective on *their* difficulties. Even in the active voice, she spoke of the insecurity she still felt at times, which she attributed to her childhood experiences of being raised in a rural area, developing concepts of God and the church that she later rejected (the 'religious façade' as she termed it), and living with an alcoholic parent. The active voice showed how Doreen took that insecurity and used it as a tool for maintaining connection with the experiences of the women she served. In her personal leadership formation she found fertile ground for developing the skills to lead other women through a similar journey with compassion and self-awareness.

3.2.3 Step 3 – Contrapuntal voices (Doreen)

Four distinct voices emerged from the completion of Steps 1 and 2 in the analysis of Doreen's interview: Transformer, Feminist, Evangelist and Leader. Although Doreen's ability to bring a positive perspective to bear on nearly every situation made it difficult at times to discern the effects of her past in some situations, it was necessary to be very cautious of 'flattening' the voices by forcing a positive tone into their narratives. However, listening repeatedly uncovered a variety of ways in which she expressed the influence of her more difficult life experiences. The majority of her stories involved the Transformer voice, which spoke about how she responded to obstacles and challenging situations. The Transformer voice also related the many times she drew on her optimistic outlook to metamorphose those obstacles and situations in such a way as to produce positive outcomes in her own life and the lives of others. The Feminist voice addressed her concern for women – particularly rural women. In the Feminist voice, she not only articulated her vision of the needs of rural women, but also verbalized how she was working to address those needs. The voice of the Evangelist passionately spoke about her faith – both the positive and negative aspects – how she viewed it, and how she integrated it into her work. Finally, the Leader voice was a verbalization of her leadership experiences and the ways in which she had taken the initiative to make changes for herself and others. It expressed her vision for her own life, for the women she led and for the organizations in which she was involved.

Transformer

This voice, more than any other, captures Doreen's spirit and leadership style. One of the most obvious facets of this voice was the way in which she seemed to be in a continuous process of reframing the challenging aspects of her life so as to enable her to see the positive in any situation. One example that demonstrates this quite clearly is that of her father's alcoholism:

> Um, looking back on my childhood it was quite happy. My father had a drink problem, so that added to the whole thing of the impoverish, you know, deprivation, no money, and things like that, but. Um, he was also a very good gardener, so there was always loads of vegetables and things like that, Lori. You know, so. There was one side of him and there was another side. Yeah. You know?

And later, when speaking of the other children in one of the schools she attended:

> They would have ranged from, from upper class down to working class. Um, suppose th- the experience of that within school was that, it was OK. But you always felt very much a kind of- that would have had an impact on your self-esteem, and your confidence. Um, but it was OK, you know, um. Suppose looking back, s-suppose I- When I look back on it, I try to not let it, you know, um, because my mom was a great knitter and so was my, so was my dad believe it or not. He was, he was good. So we always seemed to have, always nice clothes that they had knitted.

While a perfunctory reading of these quotes, isolated from the remainder of the interview text, would perhaps give the impression that Doreen was simply painting a positive gloss onto the pain of her past, a more in-depth reading of the complete transcript shows her as a woman in process, willing to utilize her developing agency to lead other women in their journeys to transform and/or escape from the negative structures of their own narratives.

The second facet of this voice expresses Doreen's ability to exceed the expectations of others, or, in some particularly relevant examples, her determination to succeed in spite of the expectations of others. Her educational journey is one such example. Listening to her transcript brings to light the impact on her life of leaving school at the age of fifteen. Rather than simply mentioning it as a fact and moving forward in her narrative, Doreen specifically states her age at the time of her school-leaving three times. The first two occurred during her description of her childhood:

> But, um, so that meant that I would have had an opportunity to have went to grammar school. But because my parents couldn't afford to do that because there would have been fees involved, I never had the opportunity to go to grammar school. So I left school, then, when I was fifteen, because that was an expectation, too, that you then go out and bring in some income to your family. So I left school at fifteen, and went to work, in a shirt factory.

The third occurred in her response when asked about leadership opportunities in the schools she attended:

> I mean, um, I would have had an opportunity to go on, in my fifth year, to do my GCSEs, but- no my fourth year, but they- I left when I was fifteen. Um, 'cause you did those when you were sixteen. But I- The way my birthday fell was in July and I was allowed to leave, and the expectation from my parents was that I, that I would leave and contribute to the, the household income.

While obviously disappointed that she was unable to continue with her schooling at that age, Doreen chose to pursue further education at a later time in her life, when the challenges were different, and, perhaps, greater. At the age of thirty-five, as a farmer's wife and the mother of five children, she returned to education. Although she cited financial need as the reason for her renewed interest in education, the larger view provided by her transcript revealed a motivation that had been in place long before the financial pressures. As noted above, Doreen's process of returning to education began when she was paid off from a factory job and saw a sign at the women's centre advertising a course in which she was interested. In the interview, she described her thought process the night after seeing the advertisement, a process which culminated in her realization that, 'I can actually take that step that I've always wanted to take, and it is now time for me'. The following quote demonstrates that Doreen's desire for education and determination to pursue it far outweighed the factor of financial necessity as she spoke about completing the first course and going on to do another:

> It was very, very intense – doing it in one year. And five children. Yeah. And we had no- I had no computer in the house and I used to have to go to . . . Women's Group. Um, used to go down there in the evenings after I put the children to bed, and sometimes because I had no computer. So I would sit 'til two and three in the morning doing my assignments. And then come home, go to bed for four hours, [slightly laughing] and get up in the morning and go to university. . . . And there's one time I thought of dropping out, I was so stressed out, but I kept in there.

The fourth facet of the Transformer voice initially revealed itself in Doreen's description of the first day of her course. This facet showed a side of Doreen that relished doing what others considered impossible:

> And I remember, Lori, in the first day of the course, and, you know, the, the tutor had went around to everybody and they said, you know, 'Where do you

see yourself in three years' time?' And I remember saying, um, 'I see myself in three years' time earning fifteen pounds an hour'. And everybody laughed. And in three years' time, Lori, I was making fifteen pounds an hour.

Later in the interview, she demonstrated the ways this facet informed her work as a leader at the women's centre as she spoke of fighting for funding for the centre. She carried the same fighting spirit into her advice for rural women interested in leadership, summing up the Transformer voice (emphasis hers):

You can do it 'cause I did. I did. I did. And you *can* do it. And I'm- I'd be telling those women in my class that all the- You *can* do it. You can do it.

Feminist

As with Alice's case study, the difficulty in terming a voice 'Feminist' is that Doreen never directly identified herself as a feminist. However, in places where her actions and words aligned with feminist principles – and those places are many – I have given the name 'Feminist' to that voice. The Feminist voice was a clearly identifiable one, given the fact that Doreen's concern for women and their wellbeing permeated her work and thinking.

The Feminist voice first appeared when Doreen made the switch from passive to active voice, at the point where she described continuing on in her second educational experience and completing a diploma 'in ICT and Women's Studies'. While she initially cited a personal motive for pursuing education (her family's need for financial resources), it became apparent that she used the courses she took to benefit others outside her family as well. Following the completion of her diploma, Doreen became a facilitator '. . . on a capacity-building course for women in the rural areas'. The satisfaction in her voice when she revealed her salary was backed by a sense of purpose in her work: 'And they actually were paying me twenty-something pounds an hour to [laughs] you know, to go out and, and outreach into those rural, rural areas.'

Doreen also spoke in her Feminist voice when she expressed admiration for the woman she described as her greatest mentor. This was not simply because the mentor was a woman, but rather because she had 'paid a big price for women in Ireland', and because Doreen recognized the impact her mentor had had on a great number of women who were like Doreen. It seemed that Doreen modelled much of her work on the ethic of care demonstrated by this mentor, and admired the mentor's willingness to sacrifice herself for the good of other women.

The portions of Doreen's interview with the largest concentration of the Feminist voice centred on the various organizations in which she had served since completing her education. Within the context of her functions in those organizations, she articulated the passion she felt for helping – 'against everything that was coming against them' – women she saw as being in circumstances similar to those in her own past. Doreen's work at the centre allowed her to teach courses on 'Assertiveness, Confidence-Building and the Power of Positive Thinking', but her focus was clearly on listening to and aiding the individual women rather than merely delivering lectures (emphasis hers):

But what I'm encouraging women is to believe that they **can** do it. That they **can**, you know, it's just setting those goals and believing that they're achievable and you **can** do it. . . . And I mean, just the women- other women's stories!

Her belief in the potential of those women reflected her personal journey and the ways in which her life had transformed. That belief, combined with the life changes she had observed taking place in others as a result of the courses she taught, also motivated her to fight for funding to keep the centre going. Further, she spoke openly about the lack of support rural women's centres received from local councils – which she perceived as being the result of '[not going] through that glass ceiling at all'. She continued to make her point by addressing the disparity she noted between the unified voice of urban women and a deficiency of confidence and disunity of voice among rural women.

One final anecdote in the Feminist voice provides a succinct articulation of Doreen's willingness to deal with the perplexities of leading towards change for women rather than abandoning both an imperfect system and the women who operate within it. After self-identifying as a member of a particular political party (Party B, below), she described attending a conference and hearing women from four political parties being asked to speak about their roles within their respective parties:

And I thought, 'I'm going to sit back from this, and I'm going to really, really listen and just think, "Well who would I vote for?"' And I mean I was shocked. I was shocked at myself. The one person I would have voted for would have been (Party A). That was the only party. As a (Party B member). You know, for a woman from (Party B) to say, 'Well my, my role is to make the tea. For the men.' . . . So I've been after them (Party B) boys since.

Evangelist

As mentioned above, Doreen's initial uncertainty regarding the appropriateness of speaking about her faith within the context of our interview quickly gave way to an almost childlike joy when she realized that the inclusion of her spirituality was indeed allowed and even encouraged because of its centrality to her self-concept and her leadership. Once this door was open, the Evangelist voice spoke freely and often. Having identified Jesus as her greatest mentor, Doreen went on to confess:

And, I mean, even in working in [the centre], Lori, I mean I see so many people that came- Like I would say that that's the reason that- this- I just think this is my wee church. You know what I mean? But I don't- I, I can't do that, but I just, it's I've just so much compassion for these women. . . . So my heart's desire would be one day to out there just pastoring full-time, but I do this in the meantime.

Thus the Evangelist voice illuminated the ways in which Doreen's leadership ranged beyond simply meeting the physical, social or educational needs of the women with whom she worked at the centre. Her desire to assist in their development extended to the spiritual aspect of their lives as well.

Because she was unable to directly advocate her personal ideas of faith in God within the centre, she had proactively created an opportunity for the women to access a course on spiritual development through her church. For Doreen, 'breaking through all of those barriers that your upbringing has brought you, and all that religious stuff, that you've been taught over the years' was the key to overcoming the feelings of insignificance and unworthiness that had accompanied her transition from poverty to financial comfort and her journey into leadership – feelings that she saw reflected in the stories of the women she led. It was her goal to make that same 'breaking through' possible for other women – even if they did not attend the spiritual development course.

For Doreen, her faith in its current form was the root of all possibilities in her life and the lives of others. It was the foundation out of which her life had been transformed, and, to her, offered the same hope for other women:

> And it's getting- it's breaking through all of that religious façade and all of that, and getting to believe in themselves that it is possible. It is. And it is possible.

Leader

Doreen's Leader voice could most clearly be heard in stories that conveyed her natural giftedness in leadership characteristics and skills – even in accounts of those events that took place before she had been trained in leadership. Doreen's thought processes were those of a leader long before she took on formal leadership roles. The first indications of the Leadership voice in Doreen's narrative appeared in her response when asked if she had ever seen leadership modelled by anyone in her family. After pausing to consider the question, she replied that she had not, and that the women in her family stayed at home or worked in factories (which is what her sisters had done). Taken in the context of the entire transcript text, this response showed that Doreen had made choices that differentiated her from the expectations of her family – a difficult route to take, and one that showed initiative and the potential for leadership on her part.

The Leader voice began to come more fully into expression in Doreen's narrative during her description of returning to school at thirty-five, as she recounted setting and achieving goals – both academically and financially – that required extraordinary effort on her part and surpassed the assumptions and expectations of those around her. Immediately following the completion of her courses, she took up a post leading other women on the same journey she had just undertaken. Doreen's other leadership capacities were many and varied: Chairperson, member of a management committee, Vice Chair, member of three boards of directors, pastor, speaker and centre development manager. As she described the diverse leadership positions she had held in organizations and the work she was undertaking at the time of our interview, the Leader voice expressed itself with increasing directness.

Doreen's greatest leadership strength was articulated by the Leader voice as her ability to create and maintain a vision for transforming the lives of other women. That vision informed every aspect of her leadership, compelling her to model goal setting/achievement in the courses she taught, and giving her a deep sense of gratification when she heard success stories from the women:

> So we kind of- we set goals, when they come in we set goals that would be seeing things happen, within two to three weeks, and then we see things that- 'Cause I only have them for a ten-week period. But they'll come back in to you and they'll say to you, [whispering] 'God, this really- this really does work you know!' And I say, 'Yeah. [speaking aloud] Because you *believe* it! You *believe* that it's going to work!'

It also allowed her to continue to exercise leadership even in situations where her professional needs were left unmet:

> And mostly the women that come on [our Board of Directors] would be at grass root levels. They're women that have been participants, on the courses. Um, so we're not really looking for women that would have skills, Lori. And yet with all, that has an adverse affect too, because sometimes you need those women in terms of support for me.

Finally, nearing the end of her interview, Doreen's Leader voice spoke both rationally and fervently about the needs of the women and organizations she served. Using illustrations from her time as a leader in the rural women's sector, she expressed concern not only for the individual women in her specific organization but also for the circumstances of rural women and rural women's organizations in general:

> I'm always trying to encourage them too. But, um, I-I just sometimes feel that we have- I'd like to see the c- the council doing more. You know the local, local cou- I just feel, that . . . we haven't really went through that glass ceiling at all. You know? . . . I still think that there's a big difference between urban and rural women. And in terms of confidence and self-esteem I don't care what kind of class you come from. I- I just think that wom- rural women are not- They're just, just- They don't have the, the confidence to actually be able to speak. And there's not that unified voice either. You know. 'Cause they're so disperse.

Doreen's awareness of these needs and her actions in working to meet them plainly demonstrated her ability to think and act as a leader, utilizing her personal experiences as the foundation from which she led.

Synthesis of voices

While very distinct in their tones, each of Doreen's voices interacted with or overlapped the others. In the majority of cases, the voices supported each other, but occasionally their conjunctions opened a curtain into the deeper thought processes involved in Doreen's development as a leader. In those moments, what initially seemed the effortless speaking of the Transformer voice could be seen as the product of many years of consistency and determination in her ways of thinking. She attributed much of her success in transforming negatives to her faith, which was made obvious through the Evangelist voice. However, the Feminist voice showed that her concern for other women was also a motivating factor. The

Transformer, Evangelist and Feminist voices all contributed at various points to her Leader voice, and the four voices together painted a fascinating picture of Doreen's journey into leadership.

The Transformer and Leader voices appeared simultaneously several times – most frequently in the places where she described major life changes and her positive reframing of those events. Doreen's Feminist and Leader voices were most often seen together at points involving her work within organizations and the impact of that work on the women she served. Interestingly, while the Evangelist voice did intertwine with each of the other voices at points, it spoke least often with the Feminist voice, and then only in the context of the courses Doreen taught.

One story that took place at the intersection of Doreen's Evangelist and Transformer voices provided valuable insight into her personality and the way she responded to challenges. The story began with her description of the development course she led at her church:

> So the . . . Ministry is more the spiritual aspect, um, that as the women read about it in the paper and they feel they want to go beyond what they're getting here – because I can't do that in here. And, at the minute we have, I mean, we have about 70 or 80 women, from both sides of the community coming to it.

And later:

> And I tell you. And they just love each other. And I get speakers from, you know, both sides of the community come in and speak.

Remarkable as it was to hear her account of facilitating this gathering, the crux of the story was an anecdote that revealed Doreen's response to an interaction that could have been perceived as negative or slighting. Instead, she transformed it into one of the positive motivators behind the cross-community aspect of the programme:

> You know, ten years ago, when I actually came in here, the manager of the [organization] said in a very sarcastic way to me, he said, 'But really what you need to do Doreen is, um, if you could get those women praying together'. I th- I walked out of that building and I said, 'Someday. You boy, you. I will be.'

Her immediate response to the manager's sarcasm and later success as the leader of the cross-community group, clearly demonstrate Doreen's on-going ability to transform negative and difficult circumstances into positive, useful tools for leadership.

There were, however, two points in her interview where Doreen did not reframe negative or stressful situations. The first was in her description of the exertion she put forth in completing her one-year course; the second was in her expression of the needs and disadvantages of rural women. Because she had reframed negatives into positives so consistently throughout the interview, these points took on particular importance. While her other stories showed a Doreen who had a strong, highly developed Transformer voice, these two points uncovered the effort that had been required in her struggle to overcome disadvantages and to turn them into positive tools, as well as her continuing determination to do so. Doreen's ability to transform her circumstances was a hard-won gift – one that prepared her well for leadership.

3.2.4 Analysis (Doreen)

As with Alice's interview, returning to the original research questions provided the framework for analysing Doreen's transcript. This analysis first examines the ways in which specific people, organizations and events contributed to her leadership development. It then explores Doreen's individual thought processes and choices – in both the supportive (positive) and non-supportive (negative) contexts she faced in her leadership journey.

External factors: People, organizations and events
As recounted in her interview, the story of Doreen's leadership journey centred on people. It was through the lens of interactions with people that Doreen viewed her experiences with organizations and found meaning in the events of her life. Her involvement with organizations provided a framework on which she constructed her distinctive expressions of enthusiasm for her faith and service to others. The most significant events of her life not only formed her, but were themselves formed *by* her into tools for assisting others. All three factors – people, organizations and events – were synthesized into an effective form of leadership by Doreen.

External factors: People
FAMILY OF ORIGIN   Doreen's parents had a tremendous impact on her life. This was most obvious when she spoke of their mixed marriage and her father's 'drink problem', both of which led to forms of social stigma. Although her father's family had been helpful to Doreen's family in providing food and milk from their farm, there was no contact with her mother's family. Having experienced ostracism (because of her parents' marriage), alcoholism and poverty as a child, Doreen's leadership was characterized by a particular focus on, and compassion for, women from similar backgrounds. Her cross-community work distinctly reflected the influence of her experiences as the child of a Catholic/Protestant union, and her efforts at the women's centre demonstrated an identification with and concern for the women that reached far beyond what was required of her by the job.

MENTORS   Broadly speaking, Doreen counted her university tutors as mentors due to the encouragement they had given her during the most stressful period of her studies. However, she specifically noted two people as mentors in her leadership development, both of them women. The first was a professor in the course Doreen completed at the university. The second had been her supervisor during Doreen's early involvement as a volunteer at the women's centre. Both of these women had modelled leadership in a way that Doreen had incorporated into her own style of leading.

The professor had (as mentioned in the Feminist voice section above) 'paid a big price for women in Ireland'. Doreen went on to describe this mentor as being the single most effective resource for helping many women in their development: 'I think there's a lot of women, like me, that would not be where they are today only for [her]'. As can be seen from Doreen's account of her own work, she had internalized this mentor's ethos and was continuing in the same vein as she laboured to assist women in achieving their goals.

The second woman had given Doreen the opportunity to develop practical leadership skills. To her, Doreen attributed fostering the skills that 'put me into the place of being able to achieve what I have today'. It was in speaking of her own work to foster leadership development in other women that Doreen referred to this second mentor. Again, this reflected an internalization of her mentor's example, and indicated the depth of the effect this woman had had on Doreen's leadership development.

HUSBAND AND HUSBAND'S FAMILY OF ORIGIN   The change in social location brought about by Doreen's marriage and incorporation into her husband's family opened vital possibilities for her to grow as a learner and a leader. Her husband's family was much more financially secure than her own family had been, and more emotionally stable as well. In her own words, '. . . it was just unbelievable . . .'. Having, of necessity, left school at an early age to assist in meeting the financial obligations of her family of origin, Doreen's account of returning to education after her marriage into a wealthy family revealed a vast difference in attitude towards academics. Of her husband's support, she said (emphasis hers):

> He was **great**. **Absolutely**. When I look back on it, he was tremendous. And even- he wasn't great around the house, but in going for [the course], he would say to me, 'Do it. Do it.' You know.

OTHER PEOPLE   Doreen's narrative included a few accounts of encouragement she received from people other than family and mentors. As a child, she wanted to become a nurse. Her doctor – whom she saw frequently – encouraged her in this, and even told her mother to 'make sure now that [she] gets a chance to be a nurse'. Later, in high school, Doreen's teachers recognized her academic ability, and wanted her to sit for her GCSEs: 'But again they would have been wanting to encourage it, but then they soon realized that for me, that wasn't going to happen'. In spite of her disappointment at needing to leave school, Doreen carried the encouragement of her doctor and her teachers for many years – forming it into the belief that she had academic potential beyond what her life circumstances had offered her as a child, and eventually taking steps to fulfil that potential.

External factors: Organizations

Three types of organization played significant roles in Doreen's leadership development: churches, educational institutions and rural organizations. Her

involvement with church and educational institutions began in childhood and had
carried over into her adult life. Rural organizations – both community development and women's organizations – appeared in her narrative after she had
reached adulthood.

As a child, Doreen attended several church services every Sunday. In her
adult life, she continued to attend church regularly, and served as a leader in a
local congregation. Her description of the leadership activities in which she took
part outside the church revealed the magnitude of the effect of those religious
experiences on her life. Recognizing that she could not speak about her faith
openly in the context of the courses she taught at the women's centre, Doreen still
referred to the centre as 'my wee church' as she described the compassion and
hope she had for the women she served and led there. In reference to her working-
class background and the position of other women in the same circumstances,
Doreen spoke of the need to '[break] through all of those barriers that your
upbringing has brought you, and all that religious stuff, that you've been taught
over the years'. She held this perspective on personal faith constantly before her
as she led other women into achieving their potential.

As mentioned above, educational institutions provided Doreen with not only
intellectual formation, but also encouragement on her leadership journey. Having
been perceived as possessing academic promise in high school, she later found an
outlet for that potential in her courses at university. Although a twenty-year gap
existed between the end of her high school attendance and the beginning of her
later education, both her childhood educational experiences and her adult learning experiences shaped how she saw herself as a person and as a leader. Recognizing that she could have been attending a grammar school, Doreen had eagerly
and proudly participated in the top class at her high school:

> I mean I remember going to school first day and my expectation was I was
> going to be in the top class, 'cause I knew I should have been in grammar. So I
> mean that was, that was a good, good feeling.

While being encouraged in her childhood education built a 'good feeling'
that sustained Doreen's belief in her potential, the university course she attended
equipped her with formal tools for leadership. She relied heavily on the
management and supervisory skills from that course in times when she felt
insecure in her role as leader, and utilized them to help her build confidence in
other women.

Beginning with her appointment to the management committee of a rural
women's group, Doreen's involvement in community development and women's
organizations had honed her leadership skills. She considered her service as
Chairperson of that same rural women's group to be her first leadership position
– one she attained after attending a course at their centre. Each year of her
involvement built on the ones before, until she reached the point at which she was
presenting courses similar to the one she once took. Having worked in a variety of
capacities in several organizations, she had developed a unique perspective from
which to identify existing gaps in support for those organizations and the people

they served. Doreen's leadership journey had brought her beyond simple partici-pation to the point of visionary leadership.

External factors: Events

There were several important events in Doreen's narrative. Her school leaving was the first, and, although it was a negative experience, she characteristically overcame it at a later date when two other key events in her life coincided: the loss of a job and her return to education. Another crucial event – her marriage into a wealthy family – significantly enhanced her access to education and, thus, leader-ship opportunities. Finally, as has been discussed throughout this analysis, Doreen's decision to take a course at the age of thirty-five put her firmly on the path to a formal leadership post.

Internal factors: Individual thought processes and choices

Doreen's most characteristic thought process was that of positivity: reframing negative events or the negative attitudes of others and transforming them into motivation for her work. The role of positivity in Doreen's leadership development cannot be underestimated, as it contributed significantly not only to her becoming a leader in the formal sense, but also to the manner in which she exercised leadership. This positivity facilitated her successes as a leader, allowing her to hold the negative experiences of her life and the lives of others in tension with the potential and hope which she believed in so strongly. Additionally, through her internalization of the successes of the women at the centre, it enabled her continuation as a leader in circumstances where she received very little support.

Much of Doreen's hope for others stemmed from her faith in God. As with the positivity described above, Doreen infused faith into every area of her life and leadership – including her work with rural women. While recognizing that what she termed 'religious stuff' had the potential to produce 'barriers' and 'insecu-rity', she also viewed religious faith as an implement for 'breaking through' such negative ideologies. Because of her strong belief in the power of God to change women's lives, she had taken the initiative outside the confines of the centre to develop and lead a course on spirituality at her church. She took great joy in the inclusion of this concept (albeit in acceptable, secular verbiage) in her courses at the centre.

One additional thought process accompanied many of the most important decisions of Doreen's life – that of belief in herself. A portion of this self-belief appeared to stem from curiosity regarding her own potential, as though she her-self was uncertain where the outer limits of her abilities might be found. Although she admitted feeling insecure at times, she repeatedly achieved beyond what was expected of her. From this place of self-belief and curiosity, she not only found the determination to follow through in challenging situations, but also – as in the case of discovering that she would have voted for 'Party A' when listening to candidates from four political parties – the willingness to have her assumptions and ways of thinking challenged. Belief in herself gave Doreen a position from which to develop self-belief in the women she led, aiding them in their growth towards positions of leadership.

Summary of Case Studies

Owing to the extensive differences in their voices and leadership development narratives, Alice and Doreen provided an ideal backdrop for examining the findings from the remaining transcripts. Several points should be borne in mind as this examination progresses. First, in order to fully hear the voices presented below, it will be necessary to remember the author's social locations as an academic, a feminist, a participant in the Christian tradition and the daughter of a rural family. Secondly, although Alice and Doreen's transcripts were chosen as case studies, they do not encompass the complete spectrum of voices present in the body of participants. This will become more obvious in the segments to follow, as some voices that were present in the case studies were not significantly present in the remaining transcripts, and some significant voices appeared in the other transcripts but were absent in Alice and Doreen's narratives. Finally, the findings are based primarily on a cross-comparison of the Leader voice as it was expressed by each of the participants. This is in keeping with Gilligan *et al.* (2003, p. 169):

> In a study that includes multiple interviews, these *Listening Guide* analyses may be examined in relationship to one another, illuminating similarities in the themes that may begin to emerge across several interviews and also marking distinct differences between them.

Listening Closely: External, Internal and Key Factors

Introduction

With the case studies of Alice and Doreen serving as baselines, each of the transcripts in turn was examined for commonalities. This process began with an exploration of the Leader voice, which was present in each transcript. From this examination were drawn the most prominent positive factors. Key Factors were extrapolated from the combination of External and Internal Factors with participants' words regarding future rural women leaders. Below, participants give voice to their experiences of each factor as it is discussed in detail.

4.1 External Factors – People, Organizations and Events

As stated earlier, External Factors (see Fig. 4.1) were influences on the women's leadership development that originated outside the participant. As in the cases of Alice and Doreen, these Factors emerged as the speakers gave voice to their interactions with other people, involvement with organizations and experiences of important events. The section dedicated to the first External Factor – People – presents the women's accounts of how their families of origin, educators and co-workers impacted their leadership journey. Secondly, the section on Organizations – External Factor number two – presents the ways in which participants articulated the influence of church and religious organizations, educational institutions and extracurricular activities/organizations on their development as leaders. Finally, the third External Factor – Events – relates four key happenings that shaped the leaders' lives and skills: 'The Troubles', negative situations, leadership training and international travel.

4.1.1 External Factor number one: People

The interview process created many spaces in which participants could speak regarding people who had been influential in their leadership development, beginning with their family of origin. Within the context of family, participants were asked to recount memories of activities in which they were encouraged to participate, expectations their family held for their future and observations of family members exercising leadership. Questions regarding the participants' years of formal education also provided a space – albeit less directly – in which they were able to approach the subject of influential people, through such categories as the social make-up of their schools, and the attitudes of teachers and administration towards developing leadership in the students. The most pointed of the questions regarding influential people addressed the topic of mentoring relationships. However, often the women did not connect their personal experiences with their conceptualization of mentoring. Responses to the mentoring question were most frequently couched in the language of friendships and informality or characterized as observation from afar. Following the structure of the interview

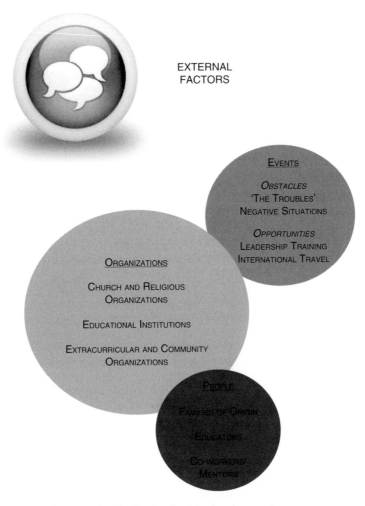

Fig. 4.1.   External Factors facilitating leadership development.

schedule, this section of the findings begins with parents and extended families of origin, and continues from there to influential educators and, finally, to co-workers.

Family of origin

The influence of the participants' families of origin on their leadership development took varied forms in the individual narratives. The categories below emerged as the most significant ways in which the participants recognized and articulated that influence. Several of the women noted their mothers as leadership models, several noted their fathers and a few noted both. Grandmothers were also repeatedly cited as important sources of inspiration for leadership.

Several of the women had parents who served as models of community involvement and/or owned a business. Some stated that their parents positively shaped
their leadership development in the arena of gender and/or religious equality.
Most significantly, nearly all of the women emphasized the value that their
parents placed on education.

Models of leadership

Seventy-seven per cent of participants identified their parents as modelling leadership and/or serving as a mentor to them. Those who named their mothers as
leadership models frequently spoke of their drive or work ethic, as in the case of
Gwen (emphasis hers):

> G: My mother was kind of a real driver. She would have been a very like,
> enterprising woman, you know, at one point had a bed and breakfast, and
> would have been the *drive* between, uh, things then. She eventually went back
> to work. When we were all up, she went to work in a local home for, uh, older
> people, in [town]. But she wasn't very happy with what she saw, so she ended
> up setting up a- a home of her own.
>
> L: *Oh my goodness.*
>
> G: And she's now 75 and she runs this home . . .
>
> L: *[laughs]*
>
> G: . . . for older people.
>
> L: *So was she an influence on you as far as . . .*
>
> G: I think she was.
>
> L: *. . . leadership?*
>
> G: Yeah. I think she was. I suppose i-i-in terms of role model, my father
> would have been a- a bit slower and more sensitive. I mean, I-I've certainly got,
> you know, inherited very good qualities from him, but, eh, c- certainly in terms
> of that drive and, you know, er, that- she would have been a good role model.
> And I'd say, probably ahead of her time, for, for her generation.

Fathers were more frequently cited than mothers as models of leadership,
many of the women relating stories similar to this one, from Fiona's narrative:

> Uh, I suppose my father, would have been a leader. I mean, father, uh, worked
> very hard. He would have left school maybe when he was fourteen, without any
> qualifications. But he worked i- in the building, uh, trade, and he would have,
> uh, worked his way up to a senior, um, (post). Um, without any qualifications.
> And he would have worked on, on t- quite a number of the local hospitals, as a
> senior (post), you know. So he, he would have always, um, suppose, showed us
> leadership and encouraged us t- to participate in a lot of things.

In cases where the woman spoke of a grandmother playing an important role
in her leadership development, the narratives often had overtones of matriarchy
similar to this one, from Cara:

C: She was the eldest of a family of eight. Um. And, quite well known in the community, you know, and people would say, 'Well how's your Granny keeping?' I said, 'Oh yes. Still fit to tell people off.'

L: *[laughs]*

C: 'Oh well then, she- she's fine.' You know. She was a very strong character, and I take it as a personal compliment when people in the family say, 'Oh your Granny'll never be dead as long as you're alive.' [laughs] You know.

L: *Yeah.*

C: So she was a particularly strong character. Spoke her mind. Uh, wasn't afraid to say things, you know. Was very strong . . . So she was, and uh, uh- she was a very strong lady, and I think probably that has had an impact on me.

Models of community involvement

While not all of the women counted their parents as models of leadership, more than half of the narratives contained references to parental involvement in the local community. This involvement took many forms, ranging from formal participation in community organizations to informal interactions at local shops or businesses owned by the parent. Maureen's expression of her father's contribution to the local community encompasses a bit of both perspectives, beginning with his association with the local football club:

Well I suppose Daddy was quite involved in the community. He, as I say, he was treasurer or secretary of the football club for, oh, 'x' number of years. Um, to my knowledge he didn't ever play football but he was involved in the management of it, um, and the committee.

Later in the interview, she gave examples of his less-formal role in the community:

M: [H]e also collected pools. . . . [H]e, he had all this network of people who paid so much every week and he, he got that all organized and sent off and then some people won prizes, so they came back and then he had to distribute them among the people and. He was forever doing something.

L: *He was an organizer!*

M: Yes. And he was a man that carried a diary with him. He had his diary and he wrote down *everything*.

L: *Oh my goodness.*

M: Daddy wrote everything, if. I remember the priest coming one year to ask him, um. Our, our area, quite a few areas here would have a cemetery mass in the cemetery during the year. And at that mass they would read out the names of all the people who had died in the previous year. Who'd been buried in the cemetery. And the priest came to ask Daddy one time [laughing] who all had died.

L: *[laughs]*

M: He wasn't sure! I mean you'd think the priest would know! . . . [laughing] So he was, wasn't just, you know he wasn't badly organized or anything. It was just, he was just checking on this one. But he knew Daddy was the man that would have everything written down.

Models of equality

Several of the women who were interviewed expressed their parents' promotion of equality in the areas of religion, national identity and/or gender. Some parents had explicitly encouraged equality, while others had more subtly demonstrated their belief in the concept. In the case of Helen, equality – here in the sphere of religion – was overtly encouraged by her parents (emphasis hers):

H: We would have been a Catholic family. Em, parents would have been very religious. Um . . . So, a- but religion was broader than-

L: *Right.*

H: It was very broa- Like, I remember as a young woman- young girl, I would have read in the local Protestant church in my town. Read readings, and we would have, you know the, Protestant, um, minister would have been in our house regularly, and w- it would have been very open. While my parents were very, religious, they would have been **very open** to other religions.

In Gwen's family's business, equality – here of national identities – was normalized through everyday interactions:

It was always a mixed community, and our bar was always mixed. And my parents would have influenced me very strongly too. . . . And certainly, my parents always gave us a message about being non-sectarian. Everybody welcome, regardless of what- w- I grew up with a strong, I suppose, a- a sense of being Irish myself and my family, but equally, people came in, that, you know, w- would have seen themselves as British. And, and whatever. And that wasn't a problem. It was just- Because it was the local pub, it was just a very much a focal point in the community.

In contrast, Eva's parents (who had three children – all girls) expressed their views of equality – here regarding gender – in an understated manner. Thus their views appeared to stem more from necessity than any driving principle:

E: Mean, I was- helped my father milk the cows and, do all the farm work. Because there's no boys – you just got stuck in and did it.

L: *Absolutely.*

E: And we were expected to do everything that boys would do.

Valuing of education

A substantial majority of the women who participated in this study portrayed their parents as encouraging and/or highly valuing education. While parents had served as models in other areas of life, education was often encouraged by these women's families of origin because of the opportunities their parents had *not* been afforded. Olivia and Patricia spoke together about their experience of this situation:

L: *So, what value did your families place on education?*

O: High.

L: *Yeah.*

P: Yeah. Mine as well. And, I think part of it was because my mom, mother and father both left school at fourteen. And it was really a case of, 'Get out. Work. Earn money.'

O: [laughs]

L: *Yeah.*

P: Because there just wasn't very much of it around.

L: *Exactly.*

O: Mm hmm.

P: And, um, you know, they left school with the most basic of education. And, um, they did everything, to encourage me to, to try and to push on ahead.

L: *Yeah. Was it the same for you Olivia?*

O: Yeah. Um. Again, father's education would have stopped basically as soon as he was able to escape. And uh. But they were very focused on, you know, you went through school, you took whatever opportunities were going. And there was never any, you know, ifs or buts about it.

P: Mm hmm.

Veronica's narrative demonstrates a similar attitude towards education:

V: My parents were particularly interested in educating the girls in the family. That was like what you did.

L: *Yes.*

V: You wanted to give your, daughters a future, you educated them.

L: *[laughing] Yeah.*

V: 'Twasn't on the farm.

Some of those whose parents were from the Catholic and/or Nationalist tradition appeared to have encouraged the participants in their education with Northern Ireland's cultural difficulties in mind, as can be seen through Gwen's words:

G: You know, a- and I suppose the message that [my mother]- There's five girls in the family and two boys, a message she always gave us was about education. Uh, well both my parents did, because, at that time, you know, er, you know- Th- their generation would have seen a lot of discrimination against

Catholics. And there was that kind of a thing that they always said, education was a way out of what they used to term 'The Nationalist Nightmare'.

L: *Yeah.*

G: So, they put a great emphasis on education.

Two of the participants whose parents had strongly valued and encouraged education had slightly different perspectives. Helen's family also placed a 'huge' value on education as 'the way out of poverty'. However, her father had opportunities that many of the other women's parents had not, and had facilitated the same for her aunt – his sister:

> My father was from a f- f- one of the first people in his villa- in his village to go to post-primary and then, university. And, and his brothers and sisters. And he actually helped put my auntie through. Um. She was, she was- One girl in the family. She was the one, when- to come home and mind the mother and father. And then, my father helped put her through college.

For Barbara, encouragement in education was a lens through which to view her father as 'progressive' (emphasis hers):

> Um. I- my father was very progressive. He had always said that the boys would- could go into the family business, if they *wished*, and they did. And they a- They left school, um, at sixteen. My father was very clear that he wanted to educate the girls in the family so that they would always be financially independent. . . . And, funny, yeah it probably was for my father's generation living and he had a- been brought up in a rural community himself. So it probably, it probably was quite progressive, um, for my father to think like that.

Educators

As in Doreen's experience, male and female tutors, academic supervisors and teachers had figured prominently in nearly a quarter of the women's leadership development. Helen, whose relationship with a group of her teachers had been extremely influential, described them in glowing language:

> H: They were great. They were my saviours, in secondary school. Because they probably had a more open approach than some of the other teachers.
>
> L: *Right. Right.*
>
> H: And you spent more time with them. You got to know them.

Not everyone who listed an academic as a formative presence in their life had such a close relationship with that person. Niamh's narrative took a less-intense tone than Helen's in its reference to teachers as mentors/role models:

> Very much so, English teachers. Now m- my English, kind of, qualifications didn't really, you know, follow suit. But I just always loved English and loved teachers. They would have been good role models.

In fact, for some of the women, even a more perfunctory relationship with teachers held the potential in their mind for impacting their development as leaders, as with Sara: 'In our primary school all the teachers were women. So that could have helped shape things . . .'

Katherine's narrative included this story of a teacher whose willingness to work outside the traditional course structure allowed her to pursue the career of her choosing rather than become a teacher, which her family and Headmaster were pressuring her toward:

> So I decided I would like to do it, be a dietician. But. By this stage I had dropped all my science subjects, which I had done for the first three years of school. And I needed to have at least one science subject at what was then called, um, Senior Certificate – O-level. So, the debate was, what would I do. Um. My aunt, I- No. I, I approached my Chemistry teacher, who I'd always liked very much, who had taught me throughout, throughout th- and, and asked him what could I do. Was there any chance of me being able to do this O-level? And he said yes, he would . . . He said, 'No. I- I'll certainly take you on and give you special classes. And try and do your O-levels.' . . . Which he did. . . . [T]he end of it was, I got my O-level. U- I got a credit in Chemistry.

Co-workers and mentors

Approximately one-third of the women identified co-workers (male and/or female) as influencing their leadership development. For some of the women, a co-worker's recognition of their leadership abilities had resulted in that woman's pursuit and attainment of leadership. This was true in the case of Eva:

> L: *Along the way, have you had, sort of, mentors or role models that shaped you or helped you in your leadership development?*
>
> E: Well I am trying to think . . . I mean I suppose, going through my career- more recent times I would have. I mean. I'm in a position of leadership at the moment. But, um, until a few years ago I wouldn't have been. And, I had a- a- I worked with, um, with my boss at the time but he encouraged me, greatly. Um. And I think only for him I probably wouldn't have been in the position I'm in. Um, he let me see that I could do it . . .
>
> L: *Yeah.*
>
> E: . . . where I wouldn't maybe have had as much confidence. So that w- that, um, my boss, a- a few years ago would have encouraged me a lot.

Others found the *on-going* support of co-workers valuable, as with Cara, who had had the support of a senior co-worker as she achieved leadership. At the time of our interview, she was continuing to turn to that same co-worker for advice as she faced quite a challenging work situation:

> Uh, I- I'm a believer in mentors, actually, and, um. I, uh, I haven't had a specific mentor, but, um, I- I mean I've always had- [name]'s always been very good to me. Uh, I've always been able to go to him with any issues. Uh, and he's that sort of empathetic person uh, that you can do that with. Um, and I think it is important to have somebody with more experience than you have, who **can** say, 'Well, look, I don't think that's a really good idea, you know.' . . . So. Uh, if you've somebody you can talk to about that and 'How am I going to

deal with this?' You know. And, so that will continue. You know. If you've a
mentor it doesn't stop when you're in a position of leadership. Um, I think it's
good to still be able to talk to others about, um, uh, issues that come to you.
You know.

Interestingly, co-worker/mentor relationships occurred apart from a formal
mentoring structure or programme for most of the women. Barbara's mentoring
experience was key to her vision of leadership, and involved a female committee
chair who Barbara advised regarding policy issues:

> And I've, we've worked very closely together and I have found her to be
> probably the closest I've got to ever having a mentor; and it's happened
> naturally. Um, and I have really enjoyed having that sounding board. Um, and
> she's somebody who's very, very principled and has a very strong value base.
> And that has really grounded me, Lori. Because I think, if I'm being entirely
> honest, sometimes the higher you go up the food chain, whether it's private,
> public, voluntary, sometimes th- the hazier a strong value base can get. And, if
> you're not grounded, you can blow in the wind a bit.

Summary – External Factors: People
The most influential people cited by participants were, by far, their family of origin. The women's accounts included family members who had served as models
of leadership; community involvement; and equality in the arenas of gender, religion and national identity. Many of the women had also been encouraged by
their families towards the pursuit of educational achievement. The attitude of
participants' families towards education bridged from the first to the second group
of influential people present in the women's narratives: educators. The relational
contexts in which the women were influenced by educational figures ranged from
observation to daily, personal interaction. These interactions with educators not
only facilitated school achievement, but also provided career-shaping guidance.
Finally, for many of the women, co-workers had been a source of positive influence in their leadership journey. Appearing mainly as informal interactions in the
transcripts, the exchange of ideas and mentoring that took place in relationship
with co-workers both instigated change and provided long-term support. Bearing
in mind the effects of these three groups of individuals upon the women's leadership development, I now turn to the organizations that most shaped that same
process.

4.1.2 External Factor number two: Organizations

Aside from their families of origin, church/religious organizations and educational institutions were the most common social locations the women shared.
As with Doreen and Alice, religious organizations were cited by every woman
except one as having played a significant role in their childhood, usually in connection with their family of origin. For some, participation in religious practices
carried into their adult lives as well. Given the level of importance assigned by

participants to this category of organization, it is the first to be discussed in this section. Second to be addressed are educational institutions. Schools and universities shaped the women in a variety of ways – from providing a place in which to identify their leadership capabilities to providing roles in which to utilize leadership skills. Similarly, participants cited extracurricular involvement in a broad range of clubs and activities as helping to facilitate their leadership development. Relevant accounts of extracurricular activities are presented here as the third and final category.

Church/religious organizations

Family of origin's involvement in religious activities was the most common External Factor among the participants. Their experiences produced a full spectrum of responses: from negative memories such as in the case of Veronica; to matter-of-factness as on the part of Margaret, Olivia and Patricia; to quite positive memories such as those of Rachel. Veronica's narrative was laden with the heaviest negativity regarding the church:

> [P]eople do what they can with what they have and do their best as parents, or, whatever- children, in [a] particular era. But I- Looking back it was stifling. It was inappropriate. And it wasn't healthy, the influence of the [church] in my life. And I, quickly abandoned it whenever I got any kind of analytical clarity about the whole thing.

As with some of the other women, Margaret expressed a normative acceptance of her family's religious practices: 'Well, we went every Sunday. It was the norm. We went to Sunday School; we went to Bible Class; we went to church.' Olivia and Patricia also shared this normative view:

L: *[D]id religion play a big role in your family, or?*

P: Call it- Yes, it would have- would have done. Brought up to go to church on Sunday. And, you went to Sunday School and, you were in the Brownies or the Guides or whatever church activities were on, and. Um. And that still, would be the case and I think that's, that would be pretty much the tradition . . .

O: Mm hmm.

P: . . . in rural areas . . .

O: Mm hmm.

P: . . . in Northern Ireland.

O: Yep.

L: *Did your- Was your family that way as well, or-*

O: Indeed, yes.

Finally, at the positive end of the spectrum, Rachel's participation in the Catholic Church had a profound effect on her life, and she viewed it as being a key to her leadership:

R: My parents were practising Catholics. I was baptized as a Catholic. And I received all the Sacraments, and I am a practising Catholic still, myself. And I believe- To me, my Catholicism is something that's very private. But it's something that I have and just believe in, and that's it. It's very hard to explain faith.

L: *Yes.*

R: But it's part of you, and it's something you believe in, and something that, if you have belief, a certain faith, then you believe other people, and believe that they can do things. And believe that there is a future for people and for communities, to develop and to grow.

Another common facet of the women's involvement with religious organizations was the development of a personal analytical evaluation of the structures and practices of those organizations. Cara, for example, took issue with what she perceived as the church's under-involvement in civic matters:

C: Now I, I just believe that – and this is a completely different theses, uh . . . [laughs]

L: *[laughs]*

C: . . . somebody else can do – that the church is, particularly, uh, my own church [Anglican] is not playing enough of a civic role um, in, in society in, in Northern Ireland, you know. They're stepping- Insular, they're more insular than, than they should be. Um. Now, now there's some, uh, exceptions to that. I know some very good, uh, ministers who take a, a role pastorally and go to- If there's a social services issue they would go with them, a-a-and things like- Which is tremendous, because I think, if you can't rely on your minister to be there for you at those sorts of times, then, uh, who can you rely on? And I think that's really good. But I, I just think that they could be taking more of a role socially, instead of just retreating. So that the faith actually operates in society, as opposed to being separate from society.

For many of the women, the church provided a framework from which they analysed gender roles. When asked if their involvement in church had shaped their ideas regarding women in leadership, many of the women from both Catholic and Protestant backgrounds quickly responded with opinions similar to those of Helen: 'Well, I suppose, one of the critiques I would have of all the churches is that women don't have strong enough role.' The spectrum of observations regarding this perceived lack of women in leadership in churches had at one side Olivia's light-hearted quip: 'Well in, in our church, women were allowed in the pulpit. Um, so you sort of would of recognized that, well, o- our outfit's a bit different to some others, you know. [laughs]' Margaret's comments represent the middle ground:

The Presbyterian Church doesn't- not at the minute [slightly laughing] the Presbyterian Church do not want women- h- don't see women with any other role in the church other than tea makers. . . . They don't see them as having the right to be an Elder. They don't see them as having the right to be a minister.

There's been some huge ruckuses here in Northern Ireland where male ministers have refused to let women ministers use their pulpit, et cetera. And that really sickens me. I'm not a feminist, but I just feel, women have just as good a brain as men, what's this all about? [laughs]

And at the other side was Sara's account:

There's no woman in leadership in the Catholic church. And that's another bugbear. And we, in the past have had some very, um, patriarchal clergy. Who have come on the altar and said, 'Women have no place in the Catholic church'. And that is, I mean, we should have actually stood up and walked out when he said that.

Educational institutions

Many of the women had gained leadership experience in the course of their formal education. Although most of them downplayed their time as Prefects and Form Captains and in similar roles, the roots of their leadership skills were firmly embedded there. Maureen's experience of being chosen to act as a mentor to a younger class illustrates the affirmation of her leadership potential by her educational institution even at a time when she herself did not recognize it as leadership, but simply as showing responsibility – a commonly occurring theme among the women:

But, uh, then I suppose as you got older, uh, they introduced something in our lower sixth year . . . uhhh, t- for mentoring the younger classes. So they did, you were assigned, well some people were assigned to a class of first years, coming in. Which schools do do a lot of now. But at that stage it was very new. And myself and another girl had one of the first-year classes. There was maybe about, only about four classes coming in probably in a year, but, uh. And then we had to go and meet with them or when they were meeting their form teacher be there or whatever.

A bit later in the interview, she continued her narrative of mentoring the younger class:

L: *So how were you chosen to be a mentor for the younger kid- was it because . . .*

M: I don't know.

L: *. . . you had been a prefect?*

M: No I don't know.

L: *It was a mystery. [laughing]*

M: It was the teachers, just. It was just a mystery. They came and they said, 'Right. Maureen, you're [mumbles].'

L: *[laughs]*

M: No, the teachers chose that. It wasn't, wasn't your peers that chose that. It was the teachers actually. So, they probably chose people who were going to do something. Like, rather than people who, just, didn't want to do anything.

Unlike Maureen, Irene took pride in her school-aged leadership:

L: Did you have a lot of opportunities to be involved in leadership of any type when you were in school?

I: Well as Form Captain, twi- two years in my five years at school. That's quite good because, that's voted by your peers. So that was quite, quite, you know, I'm quite proud of that fact. And then I was a Prefect as well.

Barbara's educational leadership experience was quite different from both Maureen's and Irene's, in that all of the students in her grammar school were assumed to be headed towards leadership:

> And it was the type of environment where we with- we were told that we didn't need to learn how to type, um, because we would have typists – we would be doctors, we would be lawyers, we would- we would be accountants. That was probably quite good, in a sense.

Extracurricular activities and community involvement

Extracurricular activities and/or involvement with a community-based organiza-tion had been a doorway into leadership for many of the women. Often the women had participated in a variety of activities and organizations. Cara, who served as the captain of her hockey team and a leader in the Guides, did not fully begin to identify herself as a leader until her involvement in an extracurricular organization at university:

> C: Um. Worked hard. Did what I had to do, you know. But I think – When I went to [university] and became involved with politics in [university], that's probably, um, when, uh, you would have noticed that. Because, as a- politics in Northern Ireland, there's not too many females involved. And before I was involved in [student political group], there was only ever one female Chair. . . . And then I became the Chair. . . . So. You know, that's probably where it started.

For Sara, involvement in her local youth club profoundly influenced her ideas regarding leadership and responsibility within the community. While she had also taken part in sport, music, debate and some volunteering, she described the youth club as 'the **main** activity that I'd have been involved in' (emphasis hers). And when asked about mentors later in the interview, she referred back to the powerful influence of leaders she had observed there:

> Um, anybody that would have mentored me would have- it would have been unknownst to them. They wouldn't have known it. I would just have been, uh, maybe looking at them and saying, 'Right. OK.' And they weren't always women. In fact in quite a few of the cases they're men. And it's going back to [town where the youth club was located]. And it's going back to the time when I would have been forming my- you know, thinking, 'What am I going to do with the rest of my life?' You know. There were men, particularly in [that same town], that, um, were pushing for community work and, and for things to happen in our area. Um, there were women too.

Patricia's family had encouraged her to participate in Young Farmers, through which she had gained not only important relationships but leadership experience as well:

> P: I would have been involved very much as, um, PRO and Secretary at club level. And then, was Vice Chairman at county level and PRO at county level. So.

> L: *Important work.*

> P: Very much steeped in, in Young Farmers, and social life revolved around the Young Farmers Club. Um. And, you met your partner, usually, through Young Farmers. [laughs] . . . Which I did.

Summary – External Factor number two: Organizations

Organizations unquestionably shaped the lives and leadership journeys of all the women interviewed. Involvement in church and religious organizations was viewed as positive by some of the women, negative by others and by a third group as simply a normal part of their lives. Many of the women had in some way developed a critical analysis of the structure and/or gender make-up of the leadership of their faith tradition or local congregation. In addition to their involvement in church/religious organizations, educational institutions provided a place for interaction with other young people, as well as key opportunities to recognize leadership potential and to develop and exercise leadership skills. Participation in sport, youth clubs, community organizations, music, drama, volunteering and student politics also served to further the leadership development of many of the women.

4.1.3 External Factor number three: Events

Several key events in the participants' lives shaped their leadership journeys. For most of the women, traditionally significant events such as marriage and the birth of children did not figure prominently in their narratives. Therefore, the focus here is on those events that emerged as holding more weight in regard to their development as leaders. The first two categories of events discussed below ('The Troubles' and negative situations) demonstrate the participants' ability to overcome obstacles. The second two categories (leadership training and international travel) present the women's accounts of opportunities through which they had been positively challenged both personally and professionally.

'The Troubles'

While this work is concerned with positive factors that influenced the participants' entry into leadership, the question of how these women overcame obstacles on their journey is a crucial one. Further, it cannot be properly answered in the context of Northern Ireland without a brief discussion of their and/or their families' experiences of 'the Troubles'. Although most of the women did not address Northern Ireland's 'Troubles' in their interviews, nearly one-third of the women's narratives did include a spectrum of stories relating the ways in which their lives had been affected, directly or indirectly, by the events of that era. The mildest of these narratives came from Olivia, who, although conscious as a pupil of the 'other people in *very* different uniforms who went [to] totally different schools', admits that she 'didn't realize at the time' what effect 'the Troubles' had on her:

> L: *[W]ould you say that 'the Troubles' affected you at all?*
>
> O: Inevitably. You didn't realize it at the time. But inevitably they did. Um. You know when you went away places and you sort of found there was a different environment out there. But you weren't conscious of it at home. That was just the way life was.

Olivia's involvement in the worlds of horse showing and cattle dealing had facilitated a broader interaction with 'both sides of the community', and she felt that she 'possibly had more contact [with people from both sides of the community] than many's another one as a result of that'. While Olivia's experiences had been limited to non-violent and even positive social interactions, a far more profound and personal impact was present in Cara's account. When she was eight-and-a-half years old, her family moved from their farm after her father was wounded in a shooting. While affirming that she had a 'very clear' memory of the event and its effects, she was uncertain as to whether it had influenced her to enter the political arena, where she had attained a public office:

> C: So it was a pretty traumatic experience for us all. Um. Especially, I think, my grandmother who, at the time, was in her late seventies, early eighties. You know, and she'd lived there all her life, so it was very traumatic for her. So, uh, inevitably, um, people ask do I think that that has had a, [laughs] an impact on my choice of career.
>
> L: *[laughs]*
>
> C: Um, I simply don't know. Um, because it's- I suppose, I was at quite a- an age when I remember things. I was eight and a half so i-i- it's very clear to me. But I just- I just don't know. I had a-a-a keen interest in history at school and what have you, and probably that formed part of it as well.

Though acknowledging the realities of the era, neither Olivia nor Cara had assigned power to those events in terms of shaping their career development.

For Katherine and Gwen, both of whom had parents who owned businesses, 'the Troubles' brought an awareness of the differences and similarities between their family's sense of national identity and the affiliations of their parents' patrons. Katherine described it in this way:

> K: And, mean, my father had a business. So he obviously drew his customers from all around the place. And I usually explain this by telling a little story that I can remember practising my piano one day. And the little book that I was practising, included the national anthems in it, 'God Save the Queen'. And I was purely practising this stuff. [laughing] It was no patriotic fervour that I was playing 'God Save the Queen'.

L: *[laughing] Yes.*

K: And the, we called it the drawing room, with the piano. It was over the shop. And I was practising. Well the next thing the door opened and my father came in and he said, 'Katherine. I think it'd be better if you didn't play that just at the moment.' He said, 'I don't mind you playing when the shop's closed. But,' he said, 'when the shop's open, I have some customers who just wouldn't be that keen to hear that. So just leave it out.' And that was all that was said. You know. Now, he may have been coming at it from a business point of view. But I think he was genuinely coming at it from a point of view, you know, 'I have people here who are good friends, and I understand they don't consider themselves British and don't want to hear that. So we'll not have it.' And that was the sort of, you know, atmosphere that we grew up with.

Gwen's family lived above her parents' pub and had been the victims of a bombing. She expressed views similar to Olivia's regarding her parents' patrons, who were drawn from both sides of the community and were 'outraged' at the bombing. For both of these women, cross-community interaction was a normal, everyday event. Katherine's interactions with her father's patrons had fuelled her curiosity regarding Irish history, in which she was pursuing a degree at the time of our interview. For Gwen, the attack on her family and her parents' cross-community openness were reflected in later posts she held: first when she was seconded to set up a trauma centre, and later when she worked in an area that was predominantly Catholic and another that was predominantly Protestant.

A few of the women's experiences of Northern Ireland during 'the Troubles' had inspired them to adopt careers dedicated to working for change. Niamh was one of those, and at the time of our interview she was serving with an organization that promoted political awareness among women in Northern Ireland. Her paternal grandfather and two cousins had been shot and killed within six weeks of her maternal grandfather's wounding in a bomb explosion. She had particularly strong words regarding what she considered a lack of openness about the realities of that era:

N: And that whole, kind of, you know, women's role in the conflict was seen as the, you know, looking after the community, looking after the kids while the men were in jail. You know, doing that kind of supportive role. But my new job is with [organization]. Um. And we deal with the issues of sectarianism and racism. . . . Now, I have great stories of kind of, you know, bonfire seasons were, I mean, we came from kind of a working-class community, and alcoholism would have been a big problem. So from you were fourteen, fifteen, we were all drinking cider, and you know, enjoying ourselves. But when it came to, then, kind of, I suppose, sectarian festivals, or whatever you want to call them, alcoholism, or alcohol, had a way of bonding our community, as opposed to- You know, sectarian stuff starts. So we would have a Catholic light the Loyalist bonfire. And a Protestant light the Republican bonfire.

L: *Are you serious?!*

N: I am not joking you. I was at these bonfires. I know this. Dragged home by my mother for a good smack. You know. But the thing is, for every one of those stories, you know, it's kind of, it's nearly papering over the fact that sectarianism is really deeply seated in our society, and, you know, people don't want to talk about it, so they're happy to talk about, 'Well in the height of the Troubles, we had great Protestant neighbours'. Or, 'We'd great Catholic neighbours'. And you're going, 'Listen, that's great. But why the hell then have we been murdering each other for 30 years? Why have 4,000 people dead? Why are 40,000 people injured – if we all love each other? Let's talk about this elephant in the room that nobody wants to talk about.'

Negative situations

As with Doreen, approximately one-third of the women had encountered negative situations that fuelled their determination to succeed and/or to help others. These negative situations ranged from the very personal to community wide. Irene's description of two separate encounters with teachers portrayed a quite personal affront, which became a source of pride when she later returned to the situation in triumph. It had also propelled her to assist other young people who faced similar obstacles:

> I: I always had this thing that, you know, at primary school it was one – my Headmistress kind of said I'd not amount to anything. You know, that kind of way- I think that gives you more of a boost.
>
> L: *It does.*
>
> I: To prove her wrong. [laughs]
>
> L: *[laughs]*
>
> I: And I had the same with another teacher at secondary school, you know, 'You'd be better off going to agricultural college'. And I think that just proved I can do exactly what I want to do.

Later in the interview, she laughed as she said, 'After I got my degree, I met the Principal of my primary school. And I said, "Oh, by the way, I got that degree that you said I'd never get." . . . And, to me, that boosted me.'

Maureen's negative encounter brought forward her indignation at perceived injustice – an indignation later echoed in the interview when she spoke regarding funding for the women's group she coordinated. This story took place during her years in a school whose pupils were divided into classes according to their ability to achieve on standardized tests. Rather than being of a directly personal nature, as with Irene, Maureen's story concerned one of her friends:

> M: And then there was a class at the bottom, as they very, very clearly told you. This class at the bottom did literally nothing. And they were left sitting there.
>
> L: *Oh my goodness!*
>
> M: 'Cause my friend was a year younger than me, from home, and she, she went, you know, she was in th- that class. And she was actually in that class. And they did nothing. . . . And it's very difficult for people now to realize that that

happened. . . . You know, you, you would hope that pe- And there's nothing! These people weren't physically or mentally disabled, you know, that they were shut away for some reason. They just, they didn't perform very well on paper . . . There was maybe only six or eight in the class. But they were really [pauses] ostracized from their own year. And like though I was a year older, but because I came into the school, you know, at my own time sort of thing, and [my friend] and I were really, really close from home. Um, and we met up at lunchtime and break time and all that. But those people were quite ostracized.

In Sara's negative experience, her perceptions regarding her community of origin had driven her to become an active leader (emphasis hers):

And I think we always felt that we **were** on the edges, um, from the parish point of view, from the council. The c- the district council area- [My town] is very much to the side. I mean the map's actually up [on my wall] and we're over to the right of the, the map. Um, in terms of the diocese, we're actually on the edge of the [larger town] diocese. So, we're on the edge of a whole lot of things, and I think that probably influenced my choice of work, and choice of study, to a certain extent. Because, [my town's] people would have felt excluded, to a certain extent.

Leadership training

Thirteen of the twenty-two women had received formal leadership training of some type, although they were divided on the value of such training. Margaret asserted that she did not utilize the leadership-specific training she had received, but was continuing her general education at the time of our interview by pursuing an MSc in Rural Development. Fiona recognized the value of leadership training, but felt that it should be combined with innate leadership abilities to be most effective (emphasis original):

L: *[H]ave you had any **formal** leadership training?*

F: Umm, in very recent years when I went, uh, started back to work, after my children maybe, or during the time I was having my ch- family, uh, I returned to work and did a few, um, women in leadership [courses]. Um. I did youth leadership, you know, when I worked [in the local youth centre] . . . You know, so, I always had that, um, good ideas and organizational skills . . . Recently would have done, uh, training for trainers. I would have done training for trainers, community facilitation skills and thing. Some of it would be, and I think it, it's, it's sort of naturally if you're a good organization or have good ideas and can do it, you know. Yeah, some training is helpful. . . . But I think you have to naturally have it, you know.

At the farthest end of the spectrum, Veronica's experience of leadership training had proven to be life changing (emphasis hers):

V: I was very lucky to get a number of training opportunities . . . Um. I got the opportunity when I was working with [political party] to be part of a delegation of politicians who went, from the North, to the JFK School at Harvard for a week . . .

L: *Wow!*

V: . . . and that was, all around political leadership. And that was – You know
of **all** the weeks I've **ever** spent, it was the highest quality training. the
deepest learning I've ever experienced, and, the most memorable. . . . So, so
I, I d- must say, yeah. Yeah yeah. I would say of all the things I've done in my
life, apart from having my three babies which is wonderful, um, I think the
learning that I've done – the training and learning and education that I've done
– is singularly the most enlightening.

International travel

Approximately one-quarter of the women mentioned that they had travelled
and/or lived abroad for a significant period of time. For all of them, travel was a
learning experience in some form, whether through long-term experience of cultural differences (for Katherine), travelling for educational purposes (as had Cara),
or in a deeper way as for those who made discoveries about their own strengths
and weaknesses (such as Irene had made). Katherine – who lived in Australia for
two and a half years – embraced the experience as an adventure, and took on a
leadership role:

I really enjoyed my two years- two and a half years in Australia. But I thought,
'I don't want to stay in Australia', you know, 'and live in Melbourne, which is
just a big city'. Much, and all, I mean, we, we did a lot. We went out camping a
lot, which was with the Youth Hostel Association. We saw a lot of the- probably
far more of the country than our relatives did. Uh, I thought, 'I really want to
go and do something very different'. So. I can go into the details if you want,
but eventually I ended up in North Queensland – right up, far end of the
country from Melbourne. Uh, as what was called Matron, of a school
children's hostel. . . . So I arrived up there. I was contracted to go for a year.
They'd never had anybody like me before. [laughs] . . . I don't think at the time
I thought it was traumatic, but it certainly was a year that made a huge
impression on me.

Cara's time away from Northern Ireland deepened her understanding of
leadership:

I never used to see myself in a position of leadership. Because to me leadership
was always the head of an organization, the leader of a political party, people
who were actually named to be leaders. Until I went on a, a Young Politicians,
um, visit to America. Washington DC. . . . Um. Uh. So we went on that. And it
was a bit- It was- We were given books on leadership, and how leadership was
much more, um wider, than what I had envisaged before then. You know, that
it was- everybody has a position of leadership. Um, so you have a leader in
your family. You could be a leader in your church. You could be a leader in
whatever, uh, sphere, you didn't have to be at the top of – a Northern Ireland,
uh, game, as it were.

For Irene, travel abroad had served as a source of self-discovery. She visited
Poland as the leader of a young people's drama team, and found great joy in com-
municating across language barriers:

I: I think that's something that, you know- I don't think you always have to talk all the time. Drama is such a great way of getting people- young people to work together. I had the opportunity in 2006 to go with a group of sixteen [junior members of a youth organization], my sister and another guy, to Poland for a week. And we were the leaders, and we went out to Poland to meet to meet sixteen [junior members of a Polish youth organization] . . . And so there that week, yes I was so tired. [laughs]

L: *[laughs]*

I: But that was great, to actually learn how to communicate a language by our- Is the hardest thing I've ever had to do.

L: *It's very hard to do.*

I: And it was- but it was so good for them. You know, by the end of the week, they were bawling their eyes out at the fact that they had to go home. You know, that's just- you know, to me that's a great opportunity.

She visited the USA at a later date, in a work-related capacity, and made quite a different discovery about her own levels of discomfort and determination:

I: I actually worked in the States for ten weeks.

L: *Oh where?!*

I: [Names city] My company seconded me. I had just finished- My manager came back after her maternity leave and said, 'Right. Now it's now time for you to go and develop your skills.'

L: *Oh very good.*

I: So I got sent- It was supposed to be six months and I said, 'I'm not sure I could cope the six months'. [laughs]

L: *[laughs]*

I: So. Without having to get a visa, I worked there for ten weeks. . . . And, you know, it was the best thing. Actually that probably developed me a lot more. Because I was by myself. And stuck in a hotel. For ten weeks. [laughs] . . . And. It just makes you think about, you know, 'I'm here. But I have to do this. I can't go home early.' [laughs]

Developmental leadership experiences

Accounts of the participants' leadership experiences are woven throughout this chapter. However, in order to more clearly illuminate the second portion of the chapter (which discusses their individual thought processes and choices), this segment focuses entirely on the women's words about their spectrum of developmental leadership experiences.

SCHOOLING YEARS   As stated in Section 4.1.2, serving as a Prefect or in similar posts during their schooling years was the most commonly held leadership position among the women. For Niamh in particular, her time serving as Prefect provided a preview of her distinctly outspoken (see Section 4.2.7) leadership style:

> And then when I went to secondary school, I, um, nominated myself as Prefect the first year. Now, this is moving from a rural, 120 kids in the whole primary school, to [town], 30 miles away. Um. To a massive, 600, you know, 600 girls in a grammar school. And, you know, you're in class and it's like, 'Who wants to be Prefect?' 'Yep. Me.' You know. 'It'll keep me out of trouble.' You know, so I was only in the door. So I think they really, kind of, didn't really know what they were getting with me. So. Prefect.

On the opposite end of the spectrum, Patricia's brief statement regarding being a Prefect also reflected her personality and foreshadowed the understated manner in which she quietly self-identified as a leader (see Section 4.2.9):

> P: There would have been certainly within upper sixth, the Head Boy and Head Girl were elected, and there were Prefects elected as well then.
>
> L: *Yep. Did you ever do either of those?*
>
> P: I was a Prefect.
>
> L: *Yeah.*
>
> P: And, don't think I was ever Head Girl material. [laughs]
>
> L: *[laughs]*
>
> P: No there was sort of- There was a- an element in, I remember in, in upper sixth, who would have been streamed off for Oxford and Cambridge. And, you know, you sort of knew that, the [jokingly pretends to cry] Head Girl was always going to be one of that set.

PARTICIPATION IN SPORT   Leadership in sport was the second most common form of developmental leadership experience the women shared. Joan was one of the most passionate about sport:

> J: I was captain for um, captain of both the netball and basketball for about three, four years. They just couldn't get rid of me.
>
> L: *Yeah. [laughs]*
>
> J: [laughing] Said, 'What do you mean – I'm not captain?'
>
> L: *[laughs] Oh my word.*
>
> J: [laughs] So. Yeah. Trained, maybe two, three times a week, so. Quite, um. It was quite hard going. All day Saturday, from nine to five. . . . I loved it.

Some of the other women were more matter-of-fact regarding their sport involvement, assigning less importance to it. This was the case with Veronica, who – although identifying herself as 'quite sporty' – summed up her substantial role in several sport teams within a few brief sentences:

I was quite sporty so I would have been involved in all of the netball and the basketball and the football and soccer and the Gaelic and. All of that. So. Yeah. I would have been Captain and Chairperson and all of that.

COMMUNITY PARTICIPATION   Outside of their school and sport involvement, leadership in religious, community and social organizations had also shaped many of the women. Alice and Doreen were especially pertinent examples in this spectrum of leadership (see Chapter 2). Tracy, however, revealed an entirely different shading of community involvement, which ultimately led to her entry into political activities. Here is the background she provided in introducing her rationale for the career choice she eventually made:

T: I had, I suppose, a very political upbringing, in that, uh, my family were, um, involved in the incident in [town] in [year]. . . . I wasn't born, when that happened. But I was very much aware of it, growing up.

L: *Yeah. Yeah.*

T: And aware of it, I suppose too, because you couldn't be let forget about it. There were times I would have got much more attention from the so-called security forces than my peers. I would have got pulled over- I would have got pulled over and stopped and questioned when my friends were let go through checkpoints and things like that. So I would have had a very- Like I said, if it hadn't been political at home, I certainly – the external political influences would have been- would have been there.

Later, she spoke of returning to Northern Ireland from time abroad 'with *high* expectations that things would be different' (emphasis hers) because of a ceasefire in place at the time. However, on her first night home, a 'fairly aggressive raid' on her family's home caused her to take a decisive step into the political process. It is at this juncture that her community involvement as a young person can be clearly identified as a factor influential to her career (emphasis mine):

T: And, at that point, I found it no longer acceptable. I'd been away for a year and seen what life was like in other places.

L: *Yeah.*

T: We'd had the ceasefire, to me there was no excuse.

L: *Yeah.*

T: So. I got involved then with [political party]. And- Became- I suppose fairly, um, fairly, moved fairly quickly through the party. . . . **I'd been involved in elections, all my life, from I was fourteen, or maybe younger. And so, I knew the- the kind of the people involved, and the infrastructure and all of that. Yeah.**

LEADERSHIP ABROAD   As with Tracy, several of the women had travelled abroad. For some of those women, this offered the opportunity to experience leadership in a cultural context far different from that of Northern Ireland (see Section 4.1.3).

As a young woman, Helen's first leadership position following her schooling was in an international setting:

> H: Emm, my first [leadership position] after school . . . was, ehh, was in [country]. I was, um, the administrator, for, uh, an organization in [country]. And I was, there was two of us, so I was thrust into a leadership role, very early on.
>
> L: *Wow.*
>
> H: And had to learn.
>
> L: *And what age were you then?*
>
> H: Twenty-one.

She later drew on her experiences abroad as a means of contributing to Northern Ireland's on-going quest for societal health:

> I founded an organization, emm, of Irish people who've worked [abroad]. We . . . looked at North, South and Ireland – global North/South and what we could learn. And, um, we did a lot of human rights work and conflict resolution.

FOUNDING ORGANIZATIONS   Helen was not the only woman I interviewed who had parlayed her experiences into founding an organization. Katherine's leadership and involvement with charitable causes and community organizations had led to the formation of new ones. In her words: '[T]here's been a few sort of charitable things that I've got involved with that I maybe, certainly, started them and would have been Secretary of them.' Olivia's childhood participation in organizations had led to her '[b]eing sort of Chairman and Secretary and PRO. Various stages. You know, from- Um. At the time I would have been at university. I was becoming involved at that sort of level within the . . . organization.' Building on those experiences, she was then able to be 'involved in the establishment of' a Northern Ireland-wide organization that 'grew out of' the Irish organization in which she had held leadership. Uniquely, for Veronica forming an organization had been an act of love:

> And when the girls- when my- I've three daughters. When my daughters were very small, um, I, I really wanted to spend time with them. And I was quite a young woman, in my twenties, at that stage – late twenties sometimes. And, um, I started- I set up, um, one of the first preschool playgroups. . . . Because I wanted somewhere that I could be with my kids and yet it was giving them an experience- Because we lived on the top of a mountain. We lived in the middle of nowhere.

Interestingly, these organizations were unaffiliated with the type of organizations in which their founders were serving at the time of our interview.

EXPERIENCE OUTSIDE THEIR CURRENT FIELD OF SERVICE   As mentioned earlier, this obtaining of leadership experience outside the field in which they were working was common to many of the participants and was not exclusive to those who had been part of forming organizations. Barbara had moved from the area of social work with children and their families into an organization that helped ensure legislation and policy in Northern Ireland was inclusive and promoted equality. She described her former post in terms of her love for challenge – something she had maintained throughout the changes in her career:

> I loved the community development work. And I thought I'd like to do some more of it, but do some more of it in an area that was, you know maybe h- more challenging, um. And so, I ended up – it couldn't have been more challenging – the most deprived borough in the whole of Great Britain [laughing]. . . . And, um, I was seconded to develop new, um, service-level agreements with the voluntary sector, um, and new community services, um, t- to help us meet the needs of the Children Act. . . . It was a huge project. And there was only five of us working on it, for two years. . . . It was massive. And I was the only one working on the service-level agreements with the local communities.

Other examples of experience outside their current field were similarly rich, and included: Ursula, who had acted as her father's business partner before entering politics; Ruth, who had worked as a full-time farmer's wife and stay-at-home mother before becoming president of a women's organization; and Joan, who had served as a project manager in the broadcasting industry before accepting a post in the third sector.

SUMMARY: DEVELOPMENTAL LEADERSHIP EXPERIENCES   The examples provided in this section display the vast array of developmental leadership experiences present among the women who participated in this study. Their development as leaders was founded upon increasingly demanding exercises of leadership in a vast breadth of situations and circumstances – both near to home and far from it. From school and sport involvement to participation in local and international organizations, and from the founding of organizations to transitioning between fields of leadership, the process of becoming a leader, while at times difficult, was for most of the women an integrated part of their everyday lives.

Summary – External Factor number three: Events

As can be seen in the preceding sections, the two types of events presented (obstacles and positive challenges) served to generate and invigorate participants' leadership development. Although not all of the participants felt that their leadership journey had been shaped by their experiences during 'the Troubles', several of them had developed skills in cross-community interaction and/or become involved in work to promote positive change in Northern Ireland. Those who met negative situations encountered them in three ways: personal, on behalf of another and in the context of community. Similar to Doreen, other participants had also emerged positively transformed from all three forms of negative situations. In the personal, they became determined to overcome. From situations involving perceived injustice towards another, they carried away indignation useful in future endeavours. And out of the perceived marginalization of an entire community, they became active in awareness raising and community development.

The positive challenges participants faced or chose to engage in came in two forms: leadership training and international travel. Those who had received formal leadership training were divided on its usefulness, with responses ranging from one participant who did not use the training at all to another who valued her training as an 'enlightening' experience secondary only to raising her children. International travel formed the women's leadership development and skills in several ways: in giving them practical leadership experience outside Northern Ireland, in deepening their understanding of the concept of leadership and in facilitating self-discovery regarding leadership skills and preferences.

Transition: From the external to the internal
Having examined External Factors influencing the participants' development and acquisition of leadership skills, the contexts in which the women lived their leadership experiences have been illuminated considerably. At this point, the work turns inwards to listen to the thought processes present in the women's narratives, bearing in mind the ever-present framework of social locations in which they – as rural women who are leaders – analyse information, make decisions and take action.

4.2 Internal Factors – Individual Thought Processes and Choices

Because all of the women who participated in this study were identified as leaders, the points at which they spoke in the Leader voice became the starting place for conversation with the Internal Factors presented as Alice and Doreen's individual thought processes and choices. Nine themes clearly emerged as positive Internal Factors (see Fig. 4.2) in the participants' leadership development: Openness, Passion, Confidence, Persistence, Initiative, Internal Drive, Outspokenness, Operating as a Team Member, and Self-identification as a Leader. The following sections utilize the words of the woman or women who best exemplify the factors to define and illustrate each one.

4.2.1 Internal Factor number one: Openness

The concept of openness here refers to a willingness on the part of the participant to attempt new things, to experience new situations, and/or to change the manner in which familiar processes were carried out. Joan provided an excellent illustration of the first two aspects of this manner of thinking. It was first apparent in her account of leaving familiar surroundings at the age of seventeen: 'Uh, then decided to move. And come up to the big city, of Belfast. I'd been here twice before in my seventeen years. [laughs]' Later in the interview, she demonstrated openness again with a summary of the attitude that had helped propel her into leadership:

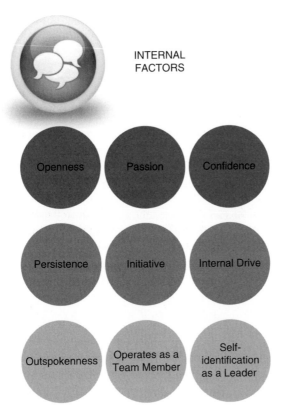

Fig. 4.2. Internal Factors facilitating leadership development.

J: I think you should always be learning.

L: *You should!*

J: You should be learning new ways of doing things.

L: *I agree.*

J: And I think that's what, um- You know, I'm never precious about trying new things.

And:

I've had no grand plan to be a leader so. It was really just down to hard work and being open, to, develop that, you know, got me, got me here.

Barbara's account of her time as a social worker demonstrated the third aspect of openness. Through her utilization of innovation within an existing social system, she was able to observe and address the need for culturally appropriate facilities for Muslim families whose children needed care:

I noted that the Asian families weren't taking up the respite care, and when we asked why, it was because how the child was handled, how it was all part of a very strong religious requirement. Muslim girls couldn't be mixing, you know, e- disabled, M- young Muslim girls couldn't be mixing with the boys in a respite care family. So we developed a service that had Asian families caring for Asian families and it brought money in to the Asian families who were doing the respite, uh, gave respite care. And then we developed a- um, a- ano- a part of a residential, um, establishment. Um, we, um, trained staff there, in, um, the Muslim culture, and how to ha- you know, the whole cultural aspects and the religion, and developed the service for residential respite. So it was just by finding out, and I suppose trial and error, in a sense.

4.2.2 Internal Factor number two: Passion

Passion for issues or causes repeatedly appeared as a driving force behind the women's leadership development and/or current leadership role. Helen, who had a 'very strong' sense of equality, was passionate about ensuring the representation of all viewpoints present on the board of an organization for which she worked:

> H: I remember when I was in the [organization], there was women and men in it. And when I'd say, 'Right. We need a su- job,' if it was a particular type of job, the women would always go for it. And then if it was to do a radio interview or to speak publicly or do the introductions or whatever, suddenly they wouldn't go for it. So what I had to do was prepare those women in advance. And say, 'Right. Today. At staff meeting. I am going to be looking for "x" to do media interview and somebody else to do, you know, the introductions. I'm going to be asking you to do it. Do not say no.' [laughs]

> L: *Do not say no. [laughs]*

> H: So it's about promoting.

> L: *Exactly.*

> H: Yeah. And actually understanding the power dynamics. In the group.

> L: *How did they respond when you, did that?*

> H: Well. Sometimes they're, 'I can't do it'. And I'm going, 'You can do it. And we- And the other thing is, we will support you in doing it. But just say yes today.' Um. Sometimes, people had difficulties. The people who always had their hands up had difficulties with the change. But very quickly they got used to that, and then we had much more dynamic, fair, form of leadership.

As with Doreen's passionate commitment to serving women with backgrounds similar to her own, many of the women derived inspiration from personal experiences and used the skills derived from those experiences as a basis for moving towards leadership. Irene's work with a youth organization was fuelled by her desire to transmit the confidence she had developed as a direct result of her membership in the same organization:

> But being in [organization], I developed, I was able to develop that through public speaking competitions. Used to get people to write the speech for me

and I could develop- I could speak it. Now I can write the speech myself, and
deliver it. My- In October past there, I had to give a speech to 550 members of
the [organization]. And that was the most nerve-wracking thing I've ever done.
[laughs] But I couldn't have done that without [organization]. The basis of
learning to develop my speaking skills, the confidence to stand up. . . . But
I think those kind of skills definitely helped me and my sister develop, you
know, where we are today. Being able to talk to people and kind of get that. So.
I just think that some people miss out on those skills.

Later, when speaking of the importance of imbuing confidence at a young
age, she continued her train of thought:

I think, you know, organizations for young people, they're so important now.
I think that when you get to my age now, you know, if I hadn't of done it when
I was younger I don't think I would do it now. . . . My sister and I now. . . help
[the young people] write their speeches and stuff like that. And the change that
we've seen in- just this past year, some of them. . . . And I think that's what the
problem is. A lot of people don't continue to, the skills, or- A lot of rural
women, who are very good leaders, but don't continue to develop other people.
And my sister and I are very lucky that we can, you know, go back and sit with
people. I'm finished [organization] now. I'm too old. [laughs] . . . She's still in
it, but we're going to go back and mentor.

4.2.3 Internal Factor number three: Confidence

In spite of the fact that some of the women made statements indicating that
they did not view themselves as leaders, self-confidence consistently appeared
as a characteristic both possessed and advocated by the participants. Tracy –
who preferred to identify herself as 'part of a team' rather than as an individual
leader – nevertheless had the self-confidence to challenge the leadership of her
political party when she began to believe that she could win an election (emphasis
hers):

And we, when I was out canvassing I realized that people were up for it. And
they were really enthused and, and could see the big picture. And every day I
went out, I come home, buzzing. Because I thought, 'We can- we can win this'.
So I had to try then and convince the leadership that this was winnable. And I
remember saying to [party leader], you know, 'Don't say,' you know, '"We've
got three." 'Cause we have four.' And he was saying, 'Well if I call four and we
don't win four then that's the story of the election'. And I said, 'You- if- d- just-
Be- Be careful with your language. If it sounds- If I'm on the doorstep telling
somebody we could win and they're saying, "Well [party leader] says you
can't".' So he accepted that rationale, and we, uh, we went out and worked
absolutely- just amazing, the work that was put into that election.

She went on to win the seat.

Barbara was confident not only in being labelled a leader, but also in her
leadership abilities. She demonstrated that confidence by maintaining a willingness

to engage in the giving and receiving of feedback (whether positive or negative) regarding her decisions:

> B: [T]here are times when I have had a manager walk in here and say to me, 'I did not appreciate what you said in division and management team. That's not how it is. And, I think you were out of order Barbara.' I have *no* difficulty with people doing that.
>
> L: *Wow.*
>
> B: Because, I think it's really important for me to say, 'Tough. Sometimes I take positions that you don't like. And this is one of them.' Or sometimes I will say, 'Well look, fair enough. Based on that wider perspective that I didn't have going into the meeting I now understand why you're annoyed.'
>
> L: *Right.*
>
> B: But I would rather, know.

Similarly, Katherine's advocacy of confidence as a necessity for young women aspiring to leadership reflected the confidence she herself possessed:

> K: I mean, I don't think I ever, you know, would have been 'one of the boys'. Certainly, as I got older, I didn't try to be, you know, one of the boys. And if they saw me as the senior person, as I was, both in terms of rank and age, well I was happy to be that. You know. And let it go at that. . . . But I think, you know, have confidence in yourself and hold your line. And don't let yourself be treated as the little woman, but equally, then don't be turned into some sort of a masculine [laughing] person that you're not. You know.
>
> L: *Yes. Exactly!*
>
> K: Sort of just be- try and have the confidence to be yourself.

Finally, Niamh's scathing caricature of what she viewed as the lack of progress in Northern Ireland's women's sector culminated in a confident avowal to forge ahead, with or without the support of a larger infrastructure:

> The thing was, I've been out of the women's sector as long as probably I've been in it. Well it's like a fucking time warp. I even left the private sector for five years and I've come back and I went, 'Are we still talking about [policy issues]? Are we still having the same debates and discussions? Has anybody fucking woke up to the fact that this isn't working? No you haven't.' So I'm just going to furrow me own plough or whatever. And hopefully the sisters that agree with me will come on board and the other ones, you play on the policy. I think it's great that yous will have that policy. I'm just going to make the inroads so that when we get there we can implement your policy. [laughs]

4.2.4 Internal Factor number four: Persistence

Throughout the transcripts, persistence in achieving organizational or personal objectives even in the face of adversity was a recurring theme. Fiona's persistence took the form of working for others, as shown in her commitment to securing funding for the women's group she headed (emphasis hers):

> F: At the minute, we're in not a great position funding-wise. We are waiting for DSD to come through, Department of Social Development, with **some** core funding. And they still haven't given me a start date . . . And, again, I'm still beavering away, trying to get programmes cost through as well, from other, smaller funds, so. . . . So we're being- we were actually packed up to go actually there a few months ago, which was desperate, you know . . . Very stressful. . . . I mean. I could have walked away from here, but I couldn't do that because my heart and soul is here, you know. . . . Um, so w- we're continuing to and we t- done a lot of lobbying on that, you know.
>
> L: *Good.*
>
> F: To try and make sure. And we're still not finished. It is all a struggle. I mean, the cities are better funded than we are.
>
> L: *Yeah.*
>
> F: But, um, I'm hoping to keep it going. [tired laugh]

For Olivia, persistence was revealed in a more personal aspect as she described a particularly challenging time in her life:

> O: Again, after I finished my degree, I went straight into PhD. And, uh, then when I had, was completing that – and again, had applied to [organization], one or two other things but had a job offer from here, that was conditional on completing either a diploma in Agricultural Communications or a Master's in Farm Business Studies. Well at that stage in the PhD, and having done three experiments, the third one of which gave me contrary results to the first two, so I had to do a fourth experiment-
>
> L: *No! Ohhh.*
>
> O: So the whole thing became protracted. Um. There's no way I was doing Business Studies.
>
> L: *No.*
>
> O: So I said, 'Right. Diploma in Agricultural Communications.' And I finished writing up my PhD. At the same time as doing that course. . . . I got married at that time as well. [laughs]

4.2.5 Internal Factor number five: Initiative

For many of the participants, entry into leadership had come through the showing of initiative. When viewed in their wider contexts, phrases such as Sara's 'So if I saw things to be done, I would do them'; or Maureen's '"Well if I don't do this," you know, "nobody else is going to attempt it"' can be seen as precipitating the speakers' current roles as leaders. Here, Sara, whose teachers described her as 'quietly confident', describes showing initiative in her own way:

L: [A]s a young person, were you seen as sort of a natural leader? Or, were you a take-charge kind of person?

S: I- No, I don't think I would have been.

L: No?

S: No. Going back to this 'quietly confident', I would, I would rather, kind of, sit, sit in the background a wee bit and not get publicity or not get the public eye. But at the same time I'm very much a doer. So if I saw things to be done, I would do them. But, I would have been involved with the community association as well at that stage, so we would have been doing things by decision. It wasn't just that I was going- decided I wanted to do things.

Although Maureen describes her taking of initiative as an unconscious decision, it had led her to the realization that she herself possessed leadership capabilities:

L: [D]id you make a conscious decision to sort of think, 'Well I'm going to step up and take a leadership role in this,' or . . .

M: Mm, no. [laughs]

L: No? [laughs]

M: 'Cause I don't think it was a conscious decision. It was sort of, um, you know sometimes they'd just say, 'Would somebody do such and such? Maureen! Will you do that?' You know.

L: [laughs]

M: You know. They just, they expected you nearly. And if there were phone calls to be made or something, it did help if you had a phone in the house, you see, so. Practical things like that, yes. But no, I don't know that you made a conscious decision to take leadership. Maybe when it came to the stage of, uh, organizing our women's group, we realized that, you know, unless we had a few office bearers in place we weren't going to get anywhere. So it was [pauses briefly] it wasn't that you were volunteering [another brief pause] to do the job. But you were being volunteered. And then, you were realizing, 'Well if I don't do this,' you know, 'nobody else is going to attempt it'.

L: Nobody else will do it.

M: So um. [brief pause] No, I'd say th- aye, that was maybe the first time that you realized maybe, that you were consciously taking on a job, where you would have to do something, to help to lead the group. Aye.

Others showed initiative by creating opportunities for themselves where otherwise there would not have been opportunities, as with Katherine:

K: And, um, I decided- now again, this, this was probably not, not common. Because, in those days you didn't have the same thing of, um, you know, people going out on, on uh, you know work placement and things like that.

L: Yeah.

K:　But, one of my aunts, who had been one of our supporters, had, uh, worked in the [hospital], uh, in the Catering Department. And she had always talked about a dietician and thought this was a very interesting job, and all the rest of it. So, of, of my own, um, initiative, I arranged during one school holiday to go up to the [hospital], to the Dietetics Department and spent two weeks, uh . . .

L:　*Wow.*

K:　. . . during that, seeing what the dietician did. So, o-, I mean, obviously, there was a, there was a- a reasonably enlightened dietician there that was prepared to offer, you know, allow me to do that . . .

L:　*Yes.*

K:　. . . because that wasn't done through the school. That was done purely by myself.

4.2.6 Internal Factor number six: Internal Drive

Being internally driven to work hard or to achieve was a factor present in several of the women's narratives. Most of the women tied this internal drive to their family of origin or other childhood milieus. Of all the women who voiced themselves as internally driven, Rachel most patently connected it to her rural identity:

L:　*So what about in your primary and secondary education, were there- Were you involved in extracurricular activities there?*

R:　No. It was very different in those days, because you were brought up in a very, I suppose in many ways, very rural areas were much more integrated and people worked together across the board, because in the farming community people pitched in irrespective of where they hung their hat on a Sunday, irrespective of political identification. And this area was synonymous with that working together ethic and ethos. But. Not, I would say- You see that sort of thing was considered a sort of ultra-trendy, leadership and that sort of thing. . . . So it was very much based on experience and what you- and maybe your inward ambition.

For many of the women who exhibited internal drive, it appeared simply in their self-characterization as a 'worker'. Like Rachel, Fiona also drew a connection to her upbringing: 'And I would say, you know, because we came from a big family you were always a worker, you know, you always, um, done it quite naturally, you didn't have to be encouraged.'

Similarly, Joan's narrative was one of a group that portrayed internal drive as deriving from identification with a parent or mentor who was a 'hard worker':

Um. My dad would have a really strong, work ethic. Worked, very hard, long hours. My mom not so much. Um. She could take it or leave it. Um. But liked to work. But not- y- w- it's strange now because my brother, and I, seem to be like Dad. So we, uh, work morning noon and night for no given reason.

Gwen, who held a public office and also worked full-time in a separate field, described her father's example of hard work in considering her own career, and laughed as she recognized the goal she had *not* been able to achieve (emphasis hers):

> G: My father, I suppose, w- found the pub- ehh, you know, it was long hours
> and that, and that I don't, you know- It was a bit of a drag on family life, and my
> father always wanted us to have good jobs and actually *not* go into the pub. You
> know, which- So, er, eventually the pub was, certainly the license was sold. And
> that, because he encouraged us all to go into stuff that, you know- Ha- He wanted
> us to have sort of a nine-to-five job and a career. I certainly have a good career . . .
>
> L: *[laughs]*
>
> B: . . . but I don't know if it's nine to five.
>
> L: *[laughs] Not nine to five.*
>
> B: It's not nine to five! [laughs] Didn't achieve that!

4.2.7 Internal Factor number seven: Outspokenness

Being outspoken, in the context of the women's narratives, carried various connotations. For the majority of those identified as 'Outspoken', it referred to an eagerness to speak their opinion on a topic or topics they were passionate about – not only in the interview context but also in their work or in relationships. Niamh – who best represented this characteristic – summed up her boldness in speaking out against what she perceived as injustice with these words: 'I suppose- I always found it very hard to hold my tongue if I saw injustice or I had an opinion. But it was, usually an educated opinion.' And later in the interview: 'Well you've got to challenge, you know. . . . You can't just accept things as they are, Lori.' For Niamh, being outspoken had informed her decision to accept a post working to promote women's awareness of the political process in Northern Ireland (emphasis hers):

> . . . I couldn't believe it when I saw the job in the paper. I was going, 'This is
> written for me. Taking politics out into the women's sectors and talking politics
> all day, and empowering women to talk politics.' Not talking Republican
> politics or Loyalist politics. Talking **their** politics. OK? Whatever background
> did they come from, they would have that spin on it anyway. But to empower
> them here. 'Here's political ideologies. Here's what the political parties stand
> for. Here's what has happened. How can you make a contribution?' . . .
> Thought it was a dream job, and joined.

On a smaller scale, Margaret's willingness to address her concerns regarding her local church congregation led to this exchange:

> M: I think there is a loss of connection with church. . . . We are Presbyterian,
> but there's a disconnection with Presbyterianism because, um, the leadership of
> the Presbyterian church has changed quite dramatically. . . . A lot of people are

disaffected. I've had a very serious chat with the ones in the Session – he would be the top person in our church, the layperson. And I said to him, 'You know, [laughing] you guys need to show leadership or the church doors will soon to close'. [laughs]

L: *[laughs]*

M: Because people have stopped going to church. They've stopped giving money. And in a small rural community, and it's only- there's thirty-five, forty people sitting in church on a Sunday, that's not going to keep the doors open. And church still has an important role to play, in a rural community.

4.2.8 Internal Factor number eight: Operating as a Team Member

Several participants expressed the idea that leadership can only be exercised as the combined efforts of a group (or 'team') of people. As with Alice, a few of these women slightly downplayed their own leadership skills and decisions, and instead placed them within the context of the support of a team. When asked how she saw herself fulfilling the role of leader, Tracy's thoughts encapsulated the Team Member concept: 'I never saw myself as fulfilling that role because you don't see yourself as leadership, you see yourself as, part of the team.' She went on to describe more fully the ways in which she undertook leadership:

> I think my, my, my- ability to fulfil that role is by listening to people. Listening to people like [my special advisor] who, who is, is a very astute strategist and and very deep thinker. Listening to people, on the ground. Talking to opinion-makers and people of influence and ensuring that you're, you're doing- as well as bringing them along with you that you're also listening to views on the ground and you're reflecting that in your decision making.

Sara, who coordinated a rural development organization, also viewed herself as simply part of a team, drawing on her participation in sport to illustrate:

> L: *And with your sports and with the- with other things, were you in a leadership position with any of those things?*
>
> S: No, I don't think I was. No. Just the youth club would have been the only leadership role.
>
> L: *Yeah. Just a team player. [implying that she had not held a leadership role]*
>
> S: Yeah. Yes, that's probably- And I would still, probably call myself a team player.

Maureen's sense of team leadership was less straightforward, but was clearly present in her depiction of the interactive nature of leadership in the women's organization where she served:

> M: Um, my main leadership part in the organization would be looking after the budget. So, which is a, very [laughing] important part of it.
>
> L: *[laughs]*

M: Because, if you haven't the budget- see d-, like, the admin has to be done. 'Cause if you don't, your budget's not looked after, and then your, uh, your funders aren't going to be happy. You have to do your work, yes. But you have to keep a strict eye on whatever else has to be done. So I would find, yes, the directors would look towards myself, and [other employee], um, for the finance part of it. They also would, pretty much, you know, rely on you to go with, whatever. You know, whatever's being done now. . . . So, it's- it's sort of give and take, between the directors and ourselves.

Not simply confined to their immediate leadership contexts, some of the other women (again, as with Alice) demonstrated the Team Member factor through a commitment to or belief in particular groups or organizations. Irene's account (see Section 4.2.2) of her long-term commitment to the organization that had helped her find confidence is an excellent demonstration of this Internal Factor. Helen's family of origin was the context within which she exercised an ongoing team member mentality, as she spoke with pride of learning about leadership, as an adult, from her siblings:

Um, and now, I'm- as an older sister you probably don't realize what's happening, but my, my sisters are real leadership models. And my brothers are. My, my sisters are, um- I would always go to them for advice now. Um, we'd be very- Go to them for advice on a lot of different things. My brothers are very strong leaders, in that they would- they're very pro-women. And that came out when I- my father died. And I remember, um, the thing in Ireland was, the men carried the coffin. So everybody was just presuming the boys would carry the coffin and it wasn't even something we planned, or- But I remember just saying, 'Well he's my father. I want to carry his coffin.' And, some people in the family were like, 'Oh no, no, no. It's the boys who do that.' . . . The three boys in our house said, 'Well, no. Of course they'd carry the coffin.' So the seven of us carried his coffin . . . And that was – nearly 30 years ago.

Also demonstrating this mentality was Margaret, whose reluctant introduction to one organization grew into a powerful advocacy and years of service on her part (emphasis hers):

I had been in [rural youth organization]. And then, out of join- that was sort of, it's not a natural step to move forward from that to [rural women's organization] because [that organization] (and today it's even *more* so) was- is seen as an organization for older women. But it was because my mother-in-law said, 'Come on'. And I went along as a twenty-two or twenty-three-year-old, I don't remember what it was but. I have never, ever regretted it. It was certainly one of the most significant steps I've ever taken in my life. Because when I went there, I became involved.

4.2.9 Internal Factor number nine: Self-identification as Leader

Nearly all of the women identified themselves as leaders. A few of the participants had not recognized themselves as filling a leadership role until asked in the interview if they saw themselves as such: 'Yes. I mean. It's funny, not until you actually ask these questions. But I suppose I do. Yeah' (Eva). In some instances 'leader' was an implied identity – as with Olivia and Patricia (interviewed together), who acknowledged their posts were leadership positions in name but simultaneously did not feel the posts required a demonstration of what they considered true leadership skills:

> P: I suppose maybe too, in our, in our current roles – Olivia you can agree or disagree with me, that's fine . . . [laughs]
>
> O: [slight laugh]
>
> L: *[laughs]*
>
> P: – there is a certain element of leadership because we're trying to work with groups to bring groups forward.
>
> L: *Yes.*
>
> P: And, very often, you have to try to show them things that could maybe help them, progress and move forward. And work with them to try to achieve, those goals. So, I don't know if it's, if it's leadership so much as, cajoling and . . . [laughs]
>
> L: *[laughs]*
>
> P: . . . and, giving them a shove in the right direction and, a bit of help when they need it.
>
> L: *Yeah.*
>
> O: Mm hmm. It's-
>
> P: Rather than leadership . . .
>
> O: Mm hmm. 'Cause the term I was going to use alongside of that was sort of like an encourager.
>
> P: Mmm.

In other narratives, the women directly recognized themselves as leaders, as with Barbara, who defined the concept of leadership in terms of her own leadership experiences in the third sector:

> B: I think- [exhales] My – and this is a very personal view and again it's not, it's not shared by, it's not shared by all, but – I think to be a good manager, you have to know how to manage tasks, how to manage resources, how to make sure that you deliver on time. And management and leadership are very, very close, but I think you can manage tasks and not be a good leader.
>
> L: *Yeah.*
>
> B: But you can lead people, and they will manage the tasks for you. And that's how I see it. That's not to say you don't take – and I can't afford to in this role –
>
> L: *[laughs]*

B: [smiling] – take my eyes off the final prize.

L: *Sure.*

B: But I think if you can inspire, and motivate, and, give people a vision, and bring them with you, and be persistent in what, your focus is, I think for me that's what leadership is about.

Some of the women had seen themselves as leaders from childhood forwards. Veronica illustrated this early recognition of leadership:

L: *Were you seen as a natural leader as a child?*

V: Ummm . . . I think I saw myself as one. I don't know if others saw me as one.

L: *[laughs slightly]*

V: But that didn't really matter. [laughs slightly]

Some participants felt that they had evolved into leaders. The narrative of Sara demonstrated this evolutionary view:

I think it's more of a thing that you, you come into rather than be trained for. I think a leader is grown rather than, uh, shaped or whatever, you know. Rather than made or manufactured, so.

The interview charted her progress towards leadership from a 'quietly confident' girl in her schooling years, to a teenager who made the choice to become actively involved in a local community association. After years of observing and learning from the community leaders around her, she then progressed to university where she studied Social Administration and Policy, followed her university education with several posts in community agencies, and was serving in what she considered her first position of leadership at the time of our interview.

Summary: Internal Factors – Individual thought processes and choices

While not all of the women displayed the same Internal Factors, many had made life and/or leadership choices utilizing the following: Openness, Passion, Confidence, Persistence, Initiative, Internal Drive, Outspokenness, Operating as a Team Member and Self-identification as a Leader. Openness was apparent in places where the women discussed their willingness to be a part of new ventures or ways of operating within a situation or system. For those of the women who demonstrated Passion, it appeared as enthusiasm for causes or ideals, propelling them to act on behalf of people or organizations in which they believed. Confidence was the second most common Internal Factor among the participants, and showed as a belief in themselves and their leadership capabilities. Interestingly, this factor was present even in the few women who did not identify themselves as leaders. The factor of Persistence became audible in the women's interviews as they spoke of their commitment to completing tasks or obtaining goals – for themselves or on behalf of others – even in the face of adversity. Those who showed Initiative did so in a variety of ways. Some had made conscious choices to take on responsibility, and others had acted with less decisiveness as they took on leadership roles in response to perceived needs. Internal Drive, in most of the corresponding women's narratives, was directly connected to observing members of their family of origin who had also been driven to work hard and/or to focus on achieving goals. For the women who most clearly displayed that factor, being internally driven meant spending long hours working or taking on work without having to be told to do so. The women displaying Outspokenness were bold in speaking against perceived injustices or on behalf of causes to which they were committed, both in their local communities and further afield. As the label suggests, participants who operated as Team Members conceptualized leadership as a group activity and/or verbalized themselves as committed members of particular groups. Finally, Self-identification as a Leader was, by far, the most common Internal Factor present in the women's transcripts, appearing even in narratives where the participant showed a degree of ambiguity regarding her capability to fulfil the role.

4.3 Key Findings and Crucial Supports

With the participants' own voices, the preceding segments demonstrated the importance of specific people, organizations and events to participants' leadership development, as well as the thought processes and choices integral to the success of that development. This segment relates these findings back to the primary query of this research: the *key* factors facilitating the development and acquisition of leadership skills among women leaders from rural areas of Northern Ireland (see Fig. 4.3).

In order to provide a more manageable framework within which to discuss the factors identified as most significant to the participants' leadership development, the findings are here distilled into five broad categories. Ordering the discussion in this way precludes the deconstruction of findings into individual, unrelated and disconnected narratives, and thus also precludes the lack of 'a position from which to speak as women, and a collective basis for struggle' resulting from that deconstruction (Jackson, 1993). However, continued integration of the women's voices will also aid in averting the opposing pitfall – essentialist thinking that masks the differences in the participants' narratives (Little and Panelli, 2003) – through illustrations of ways in which the Key Factors influenced participants' unique and individualized leadership development.

4.3.1 Returning to the case studies

In this return to the case studies, the Key Factors to leadership development drawn from Alice and Doreen's narratives serve as starting points for a dialogic

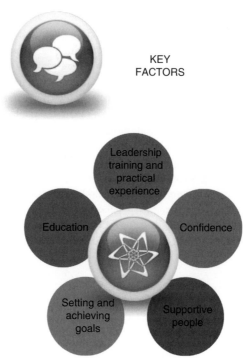

Fig. 4.3.   Key Factors facilitating leadership development.

response – inclusive of all the participants' voices – to the primary research question as it interacts with feminist theories and broader rural sociological research. Below, I provide a brief summary of the Key Factors emerging from each of the case studies.

Key Factors emergent in the case study of Alice

The Internal and External Factors facilitating Alice's leadership development can be distilled into the following Key Factors: Family, Education and Organizations. In each of these areas, Alice recounted receiving encouragement and valuation. Building on the foundation of her family's positive support, Alice was enabled to take advantage of many opportunities to be involved with community organizations and to further her education. In each stage of her life – childhood, young adulthood and adulthood – she (at points apparently subconsciously) made choices and/or seized opportunities within these three areas which honed her natural leadership abilities. Despite not viewing herself as a 'leader', Alice derived from these experiences the confidence to conceptualize herself as a deserving and capable individual in her occupational role and had become an advocate for activities and organizations that she viewed as positively shaping her life.

Key Factors emergent in the case study of Doreen

The Key Factors to Doreen's development as a leader were also both Internal and External. First, her ability to reframe negative situations and form them into skills for leading others in their own journey of leadership development – labelled in the case study as positivity[16] – had enabled her to make decisions that, while often difficult, ultimately led to her taking up of leadership responsibilities. In addition to this Key Internal Factor of Doreen's leadership development, the role of Key External Factors including women's centres, educational institutions and her family cannot be overlooked. Without the women's centre in her area, there would have been no development course offered to Doreen. Without the university, she could not have continued on to pursue her diploma and further leadership training after taking the development course. Without both the change in social position brought about by her marriage and the subsequent encouragement of her husband, Doreen would most likely not have returned to education or, alternatively, might not have completed the course she began.

Despite facing a myriad of obstacles in her childhood, difficult decisions in adulthood and challenging circumstances throughout her leadership journey, Doreen was a highly effective leader. Using the experiences of her life as tools for helping other women facilitated her achievements as a leader. It also brought meaning to negative situations in her life and the lives of others, thus providing her with the encouragement and determination she needed to continue her work.

4.3.2 Discussion: Key Factors emerging from all interviews

The case studies of Alice and Doreen provided an in-depth view of two quite dissimilar narratives of leadership development. In holding the remaining interviews in dialogue with Alice and Doreen, five Key Factors emerged: Supportive People, Education, Leadership Training and Practical Experience, Setting and Achieving Goals and, lastly, Confidence. These Key Factors were present in each of the narratives, appearing in various forms as facilitative supports in the women's leadership development. As with the presentation of the broader findings of this study, the women's own voices speak here to define and clarify the Key Factors.

Key Factor number one: Supportive People

In total, more than half of the women highlighted the importance of supportive people to aspiring leaders' development. These are compiled into three groups: Family, Mentors and Other Connections. Here, Family refers to both the participants' families of origin and their current family situation. Mentors include relationships both formal and informal in which the participant had access to a more experienced leader to receive advice and feedback, as well as encouragement in their leadership endeavours. Finally, Other Connections refers to the recommendation made by several participants that aspiring rural women leaders should network and connect with any other supportive people they may come into contact with. I begin my discussion of supportive people with participants' receipt of support from their families.

FAMILY   Recent literature (Avolio *et al.*, 2009) has proposed the family of origin as a primary source for confidence building leading to the taking up of leadership roles. Northern Ireland, in particular, has a strong culture of seeking support from family – even to the exclusion of seeking support elsewhere (Daly and Dowds, 2005). This was clearly reflected in the participants' descriptions of families of origin and current families (spouse or partner and/or children) as the most influential group of people in their leadership development. Helen very directly cited family as one of the key supports for her leadership:

> L: *How do you receive leadership support, or from where do you receive support for what you do?*
>
> H: My partner . . . I'm married to a very, a man who is very pro-equality.

Veronica named her grandmother and mother as supportively influential in her progress towards leadership:

> We're a family of matriarchs. I had the most wonderful grandmother. Absolutely most wonderful grandmother. Whom I loved to bits. And she was, you know, always interested in what you were doing, and. Um, always encouraging you to, forge ahead . . . And my mother was just wonderful as well, I have to say. And still is. My mother's still alive . . . She's a great role model . . . She just- She just- she's quite an independent person. And I think she fostered that independence in her, in her family . . . So yeah. Role models were huge, huge, huge. Yeah.

Ruth, who said she had not received encouragement from her family of origin, nevertheless cited it as a foundational support for aspiring leaders:

> Well I, I think at home- I think it needs to start at home 'cause I encouraged my own children – none of them have done anything, dramatic like – but I would have s- praised them when they done something . . . You need to encourage your children.

MENTORS   As noted in Section 4.1.1, the majority of the women did not have formalized mentoring relationships. With that in mind, it is interesting to note that more than one-quarter of the participants specifically listed mentoring among the types of support they would like to see aspiring leaders receive. In the context of Northern Ireland, mentoring has been recommended by at least one other study as a measure for facilitating the entry of rural women into positions of leadership (Macaulay and Laverty, 2007). Mentoring has been demonstrated to be one of the most effective forms of leadership development – most notably when the mentor is willing to interact with the mentee beyond the formal requirements of training curriculum (Solansky, 2010). For many of the women, this availability of someone supportive and understanding to speak to was one of the most significant facets of the mentoring process. Cara aptly summed up this desire for simple connection:

[W]e can talk about structures and formal structures and quotas and all of that. But, uh, I think sometimes more importantly is the fa- is the feeling that if a female Councillor has an issue, she comes and has a chat. And feels comfortable, uh, about doing that, you know.

This was echoed in Maureen's narrative, as she described the help she received from a mentor:

But she was of great – value [laughs] to me, whenever I started work here. Because I knew, anything, like she told me, like 'Anything you want to ask me, just ask'. And it was so handy that she was still here, in the town, working in a community organization as well. 'Cause if you have somebody- You know . . . some of our Directors, like they're, they're nurses or they're whatever. And you just can't ring that person up at, in the middle of the day, to say, 'You know, I need a bit of advice on such and such a thing'. You can't do that because they're in their own job, and. But she's in the same line of business as ourselves and she was always there at the end of the phone. I think she was a great mentor person for me when I came into the job.

OTHER CONNECTIONS   While both mentors and family members had provided much-needed support for the women in this study, participants also cited relationships in other contexts as providing support for aspiring or current leaders. Veronica suggested that the source of support was not as important as the support itself:

[Aspiring rural women leaders] need, uh, positive people around them, they need people who are going to encourage them . . . Nice, just people who can tell them they can do it, and- provide them with the opportunity to do it.

Other participants took this idea further and expressed a willingness to provide reciprocal support. Helen did this by turning her supportive voice outwards as she gave advice for aspiring leaders, saying:

[B]uild alliances. So you're doing it, with other people . . . people who support you rather than people who knock you. And stand up for other people that you're seeing- I would always challenge someone if I see that there's always little put-downs, their little jokes. . . . sometimes it isn't only a joke.

Finally, Katherine's view of leadership as an interactive and supportive connection with followers (Ladkin, 2010) expressed what many of the women also articulated:

I always feel the important things are that you're accountable and you're responsible, that if something goes wrong, even if you could point at somebody else down the line and say, 'That was their problem', or 'That was their fault', to me, that was my responsibility. . . . I think you do have to try and make sure that people are clear about what they're doing. . . . You know, rather than having people working *for* me, I never saw myself – although I know they referred to me as the boss – I could never see myself as the boss. To me I was, I was certainly the senior person, but they were all very important to me. And I mean, my line was, I couldn't have been successful alone in what we achieved. You know, all those other people were, were, were important. So therefore you had

to work with them. And I was happy to take advice from, from any of them. . . .
And I think treating people, treating everybody with respect, regardless of what,
of what grade they're at, I think it's important for a leader to be able to do that.

Key Factor number two: Education

In light of the importance placed upon education in nearly all of the women's
families of origin, it is unsurprising that many of them viewed the schooling process as a stepping stone in their leadership journey. Concordantly, research conducted in Northern Ireland has named education as a primary site within which
to challenge gendered stereotypes of leadership, thus encouraging young women
to pursue positions of seniority within organizations (Breitenbach and Galligan,
2004). Irene – who had integrated her personal leadership development into her
role within a youth organization by assisting young people in building confidence
– eagerly promoted education as an opportunity to encourage students to engage
in leadership at the earliest possible age:

> But I just think, it does work, in primary schools first, here. Encourage [them]
> to develop, you know. And even at secondary school, you know at age eleven
> and twelve. You're very impressionable. And so many, you know, you would
> notice fourteen-, fifteen-year-olds, it's not cool anymore. 'Let's, let's forget it,
> we'll do something else.' . . . But, yeah, I think it's really at school age. If you
> can get them at school age, and encourage that.

Helen's mandate for aspiring leaders broadened from Irene's personal motivation and reflected the attitude of many families who viewed education as a
means to a different or better way of life for their children:

> Well first of all, get educated. Because once you're educated it's much harder
> for them to discriminate and there's plenty of people that'll want to. Em. So,
> the more- the better educated you are, the better.

Extending even further than family concerns, Cara's focus on civic leadership stressed the need for mainstreaming leadership training so that young people
would be able to learn, through their schools, the way in which Northern Ireland's
political system functioned:

> I do take the view that there should be mainstreamed, for leadership; so instead
> of just having young women looking at leadership, should be younger people
> looking at civic involvement in politics . . . But actually, participation in the
> society so that when you talk to them, they know about the political system.
> Because they should do. As they do in America. They know about how to get
> to be President and all of those things, you know. Um. Where there's been a
> disengagement here because of the conflict. Understandably. And people didn't
> want to know, because it wasn't really, the done thing. You know. And I think
> we will get over that, as time passes. But it'll take a, a little time.

Key Factor number three: Leadership Training and Practical Experience

Although several participants advocated leadership training as beneficial to leadership development, a number of the women valued practical experience over

formal leadership training. The importance of a both/and approach to these aspects of leadership development has been recognized in recent literature (Grint, 2007). Katherine's view of the leadership training process represented a few of the women who integrated the two:

> [Y]es, there would have been management training courses that you went on. A lot of them to me, I must say, were common sense. [laughs] You know? Is how I would have seen it. But, you know, a lot of that, I mean while it may be common sense, it actually, it helps you and it reassures you that, well, what you would probably do instinctively is the right thing to do. So, yeah . . . I would use those.

Following Confidence, practical experience in leadership activities ranked next highest in the number of participants advocating its necessity for the development of aspiring rural women leaders. For many, such as Barbara (who did advocate leadership training), this reflected their view of training as having a 'theoretical' focus (emphasis hers):

> I'm also a firm believer in, um, what some people call active learning. But, sometimes I think training can be very theoretical, but to lift somebody and put them into an organization for a week, to show how it's done. Go into a political party for a week. See how political parties work. The good and the bad. . . . That also helps, young women in particular, to identify, '*Love* [to] go into politics. I want to be there.' Or, 'No, that's not for me'.

Irene turned her view of the necessity of practical experience for leadership outwards, and spoke on behalf of workers 'on the shop floor':

> I'm not sure if it's in every company in Northern Ireland, but I think some people place too much onus on education. And don't think the people who work on the shop floor actually have the skills. And I can see so many people who would have leadership skills if given the opportunity. And they have been discouraged, because they think they're not worth it. You know, they get paid crap money. . . . I hate this- people sitting in meetings deciding everything for everybody else, and never asking.

In a similar vein, Eva noted (emphasis hers):

> I think either you've either- are able to [be a leader] or you're not. I think you *can* learn as you go along, and learn by mistakes maybe you've made. . . . Sometimes, I think a lot of it is just learning by experience. I don't think you really can say, 'Right. To be a good leader you need to do this, this and this.'

COMMUNITY, YOUTH, RELIGIOUS AND WOMEN'S ORGANIZATIONS   For the many women whose leadership development took a path through community, youth, religious and/or women's organizations, these organizations not only provided them with social outlets, but also facilitated the exercise of leadership skills in practical ways and helped propel them into further leadership roles (Bono *et al.*, 2010). As the case study of Alice, in particular, demonstrated, conceptualizing the self as leader began for several participants within the context of such organizations (see Section 3.1.2 above). Oppositely, others of the women found that the organization recognized their leadership skills, as with Ruth, who said, laughingly, 'I wasn't long in these things 'til I got jobs'. This is in keeping with a 2007 study on the rural women's sector in Northern Ireland, which highlights leadership skills as being considered one of the 'most important skills' on management committees for rural women's organizations (Macaulay and Laverty, 2007).

Both Alice and Ruth's narratives reflected the impact of community involvement on leadership development that Helen cited as necessary for aspiring leaders: 'Do your voluntary work and get experience. Because, I know as an employer myself, if someone is equal and then you've done voluntary work, well you- that shows something.' Doreen's narrative illustrated the ways in which initially peripheral involvement in a women's organization (taking a course) led to her position of leadership in the women's sector and, in turn, her work in developing other women leaders both within and outside the framework of the women's centre. This is consistent with literature claiming that women's involvement in Northern Ireland's Women's Networks leads to increased involvement in other aspects of community life as well (Shortall, 2008).

It is interesting to address Kreimer's (2004) appraisal of occupations in which women are predominant in the context of such rural women's groups. While Kreimer purports that the majority of female-predominant occupations offer little in the way of training and advancement, rural women's groups in Northern Ireland often serve uniquely as platforms for women to exercise leadership in interaction with broader audiences as the women represent (and – at times – fight for) what they experience as valuable. This was the situation in which Maureen found herself and her group, as they (like many other women's groups) appealed for funding and better representation on local councils and in the Local Action Groups that were forming at the time:

> I know I've gained a- a *lot* of experience since I came into this job. And the other women- like, there are women in networks from years before I was ever in a network. And they're there. They have all of that *wealth* of experience. And they could put it to good use, *if* the funding was there . . . Uh, I do feel strongly about, uh, the local councils. They just don't acknowledge that you even exist. . . . I know what's going to happen! They'll have about- They'll decide that, 'Right. By next month everybody has to have [a] Local Action Group.' So they'll be taking whoever they can get . . . Rural women are going to miss out . . . I know we have [the Northern Ireland Rural Women's Network] now fighting on our behalf. And they have a good link to [The Department of Agriculture and Rural Development] 'cause DARD fund them. So- We, are hoping and hoping and hoping that there will be something. [laughing] It's not an awful lot it- th- that would be needed, in all honesty, to keep things going but. If you had the right representation on a board, like that. There might be a chance.

As can be seen from this discussion, a variety of organizations had provided opportunities for participants to develop and practice leadership skills. However, none was presented as more formative in their narratives than educational institutions.

EDUCATIONAL INSTITUTIONS AND PARTICIPATION IN SPORT   The leadership exercised by participants in their schooling years was foundational to the skills they continued to display in their leadership as adults. While the offices of Prefect, Form Captain, Class Mentor and other similar posts had been elemental for many of the women's leadership formation (see Section 4.1.2 above), their educational leadership experiences were not limited to those areas. A relevant segment of one recent report on young women's life experiences in Northern Ireland – while primarily focused on addressing the negative/problematic experiences of young women participating in sport and physical education in schools – cited a high number of young women claiming enjoyment of sport and also noted participation in sport as encouraging engagement in formal educational activities (McAlister *et al.*, 2007). Many of the women in this study had positive experiences of participation in sport, serving as captains of teams or in other leadership positions. This was the case with Helen, whose involvement in her school's sports programme reflected a breadth of practical leadership learning opportunities:

> [I managed] all the teams in the school, working with the [Physical Education] teachers. . . . Wasn't just in class. You travelled to matches. So I would have been organizing events, organizing sports days, working with the basketball teams, travelling with the teams . . . Brilliant. Brilliant. Learned an awful lot from it.

Aside from sport, participants also cited several other education-related activities as formative of leadership skills. Ursula – who was holding a public office at the time of our interview and had participated in student government in university – identified writing, analysis and speech/drama as most useful in her leadership development. Similarly, Niamh – whose outspokenness served her well in her role as a political educator – identified participation in school dramas as her earliest leadership opportunity:

> In primary school, I was the narrator for the whole Christmas concert. So, on and off the stage for three hours. I just was fabulous. Loved it . . . And then, any kind of school plays then that were going on at the end of the year, you know, I'd have been narrating. Or, you know, getting involved.

As can be seen from these narratives, experiences of leadership within educational institutions provided many outlets that prepared participants for leadership in a variety of other arenas, including roles of leadership that they had assumed as adults.

CURRENT EMPLOYER   Several of the women noted their current employer as a source of support for their leadership development and/or as providing opportunities for moving into leadership. Three of the women were particularly positive in their assessments of the provision of support by organizations with which they were involved. Helen's description of her political party's support as 'active' energized her as she faced obstacles, and provided a space within which she was free to make choices regarding how she would direct that energy (emphasis hers):

[Our party] have got very **strong**, em, leadership models. Very **strong** practices that are supportive of women . . . and, we've got a leadership . . . who tolerates no inequality. And is an active supporter of equality. Of women. Of young people. Very strong on that. Which is great. And you really feel supported. Because every- everywhere you go, there's anti-women. And there's misogyny. Um. But if there's leadership and challenging it, it's fantastic. It's just, it's such a relief. Because as a woman it gives you freedom, and also, it means your energy isn't wasted fighting every single battle. Because as a woman, every day we have to pick battles. That we fight.

Patricia attributed her organization's supportiveness to the differences she perceived in public and private sector work:

I think in industry it's different, when they look at a woman and think: um, maternity leave. And think, 'Oh she'll stay with us for a few years. We'll train her and she might be gone after that. Um. She'll want more flexible working hours.' And I think maybe they see that as being, more difficult. Whereas the [organization], would be very accommodating. With th- things like sick leave, part-time working, flexible working. And I, I honestly think that, you know, y- if, if an organization gives you the scope, and gives you that bit more flexibility, they can get so much more, out of you, as a person.

Finally, Veronica voiced herself as positioned within the organization as a facilitator of support for women (emphasis hers):

[T]he layer of middle management is, practically all women. And. That's wonderful. Uh. Absolutely wonderful. And it presents an organizational challenge, which is they are all of childbearing age. And will all – welcomingly – go off to have their babies. And they deserve a year off. And I have **been** that person campaigning with my banner for a year off for women having a baby. And. It's not about that. It's not about they shouldn't have their rights and it should- that people shouldn't have time with their babies. But organiza- tionally we've actually begun to be a- we- we've begun, conversations around, 'How are we going to manage this situation?' It's not- it's not a gender-biased question. It's an organizational planning question. . . . So that, in actual fact, women can then go off and have their babies in comfort.

The organizations that these three women represented were portrayed by them as having enacted supportive practices that were in opposition to literature presenting organizations as less-than-likely to offer women – in this case, women of childbearing age – opportunities for advancement (Kreimer, 2004), because their 'core business practices' (Westenholz _et al._, 2006) have not been affected by wider social issues. In the lived experiences of Helen and Patricia, this was not the case. Further, Veronica's position of leadership provided her with a platform from which she was working to change organizational practices around the attainment of senior-level leadership positions by women. Through their framing of organizational practices as positive, these three narratives provide a transition from the discussion of the more external of the Key Factors to the final two Key Factors, which are of a more internal nature.

Key Factor number four: Setting and Achieving Goals

> Oh go for it. [laughs] Uh. But . . . it wouldn't probably be easy. Uh, you would, uh, find a lot of difficulties and be prepared for the difficulties. Uh. Don't get knocked down at the first hurdle. There are times you have to stand up, and be counted, I suppose as they would call it. And if you believe in a thing strong enough, you'll go on and do it.
>
> -Ruth

As Ruth's words suggest, rural women who aspire to leadership are faced at times with a difficult journey. The three facets of the fourth Key Factor outline ways in which participants utilized having a vision for what they would like to achieve, being persistent in pursuing that goal and maintaining openness to unexpected ways in which the goal might be met or reframed to overcome their difficulties. As noted by Conner and Strobel (2007), the process of identifying goals may take time, but is especially crucial to young women's leadership development. Therefore, the following sections discuss how, having successfully implemented these strategies in their own lives, participants encouraged other aspiring women leaders to do the same.

VISION   In describing herself, her brothers and her sisters as 'go-getters' – many of whom operated their own businesses – Fiona provided a particularly vivid illustration of vision as a hallmark of leadership:

> I think there's that goa- that, um, you want to go out there and do something, you know, and, um, organize it in maybe the way you want it, or d- put your ideas into practice, um. I'm not sure if it's that, uh, if you're working for somebody else that, um, you can't ex- if you're not allowed to express your ideas or move forward, you know. You need to actually get out and do your own thing; so I think that's part of leadership too.

Her assertion that putting 'your ideas into practice' is part of leadership confirms Day's (2000) assertion that leadership development is made more effective when contextualized within specific experiences that offer opportunities to attain goals.

Joan's advocacy of vision as requisite for aspiring leaders demonstrated a coalescence of the viewpoints expressed by participants in a study of young women in Northern Ireland. The narratives of the young women included those who cited enjoyment of their current employment situation as a motivating factor for seeking out further education and training in order to progress within their chosen field, and also included those who accepted women's ability to simultaneously function aptly as mothers and employees (McAlister *et al.*, 2007). In Joan's estimation, vision was not only a means of creating the type of career path that aspiring leaders would like to have, but also a healthy personal life (emphasis hers):

> I probably would advise them *to* plan. Um. To see a vision. To know where they wanted to be. Um. And I think that- you know, in terms of, uh, in terms of

family *and* work um. You know, I think it's important to know the values and, the home that you want to have for your family and then you work to get it. Um, so that you get a work–life balance. But also to [whispers] enjoy yourself. [speaks aloud] And the people [who] take themselves too seriously, you know? Not, really up for that kind of, you know, status-driven, 'This is my territory'. And. I ha- you know, I haven't seen it work, for many people. . . . [t]hey end up very lonely. [laughs] 'Cause you get your status and you get your area, but you've not too many wanting to share it with you.

Although having vision was articulated as pivotal for aspiring leaders, it was no guarantee that the vision would be achieved. As will be shown in the next segment, the women also voiced the necessity of persistence in their attainment of goals.

PERSISTENCE: PASSION AND POSITIVITY   The essence of this factor was exposed in the speakers' willingness to forge ahead in work they considered important, though it took many forms in the women's narratives. This dedication has been identified by Elliott and Stead (2008) as stemming from 'passion borne of experience' (p. 172), and thus it is unsurprising that the work in which the women showed persistence was often connected in some way to their personal identity. Irene's desire to have 'letters after her name' helped her stay focused on the goal of completing a degree:

I: I could have finished my education at [tech school] and said, 'Right. That's enough. I want to get a job.' I kind of kept thinking, 'I just want there to be letters after my name'. [laughs]

L: *[laughs]*

I: You know? That was all it was. You know. I've got a shot. Let's have a go. And it was just to get three letters after my name. Of course I never use them now, but apart from that.

L: *Doesn't matter! What was it that made you want that so much?*

I: I, I don't, I don't know. I just kind of thought, you know, 'I'll get, get them'. Really, that's- the point was three letters after my name. You know, that was all that it came down to. [laughs]

Elliott and Stead's (2008) findings also recognized the importance of 'doing something that matters' to leaders' persistence. For Rachel, this was the foundation of her advice to aspiring rural women leaders:

I just went on ahead, and did my work. It's as simple as that. . . . And it's nothing to do with are you from a rural or an urban community. But it's just believe- If you believe in something, you have conviction and you have faith in yourself, and faith in what you believe in and what you're champion[ing]. I think that is half the battle.

OPENNESS   Focus on goals that mattered to them created spaces in which many of the women expressed openness to the unexpected on their leadership journey.

This idea of openness was close in nature to Doreen's positivity in that it provided a means of viewing life circumstances from multiple perspectives. Grint (2007, p. 242) characterizes such positive 'reframing' of situations as key to leadership development. Fiona's advice to aspiring leaders was indicative of this recognition of the opportunities presented by the changeability of circumstances: 'Well, I would advise them to, to take, uh, to be open to any opportunities that come along, at all. And that's the way it happens.' Similarly, Margaret's willingness to be open to the unexpected was demonstrated through her account of a speaking engagement in which she related the story of a teacher who had scoffed at her dream of becoming a dentist:

> And I said, 'You know, it changed my life and I wouldn't have had the same opportunities. In one way, I missed out on a career that I wanted to pursue. But then in another way, I had wonderful opportunities that I would never have had, had I been a dentist.'

For Tracy, who held a public office, openness meant having her expectations exceeded:

> Politics when I was growing up was for- old men . . . So, for me, the, the, the demographics of political leadership wasn't- I didn't fit in with that. So- never thought that I would aspire to it. So that is also a message that I would send out to, to young women. And especially young women from rural areas. You know, it, it is doable.

Finally, Helen's proactive view of openness summarized the way in which aspiring leaders could utilize it for their development: '[I]f someone says, "Will you do 'x'?", don't say "Oh no I can't do that." Say, "No problem. But I would need- I will need this, this and this to help me do it."' The confidence displayed in her conceptualization of openness leads us into a discussion of the fifth and final Key Factor.

Key Factor number five: Confidence (Belief in Self)

> Take no shit from anyone.
>
> -Helen

As mentioned in Section 4.2.3, Confidence ranked among the Internal Factors that most influenced the participants in their journey towards leadership. Macaulay and Laverty's (2007) study confirmed this valuing of self-confidence among rural women as it pertained to participation in public leadership (p. 18). Although Cara's view of young rural women indicated that she felt they were less inhibited than older women in rural areas (which she attributed to the younger women's availing of the Internet and improved transportation), the majority of participants cited a need for confidence-building measures among rural women. Fiona, who was from a 'farm family', and had experienced a schooling context in which rural children were not encouraged forwards in their education, advocated confidence-building programmes as a means of supporting young rural women aspiring to leadership. In her words:

[I]t doesn't matter if they haven't got their 11+ or if they've failed an exam. That's not, I mean it's, as I always say, 'God they- You have so many years ahead of you yet,' you know. I mean [laughs] . . . 'You can study anything. You can t- try anything, you know. You don't have to be r- brilliant at everything, you know.' So, just t- t- to keep on at it, you know and believe in themselves, you know. They can do it, if they want to. [laughs]

Rachel also viewed confidence and assertiveness as areas in which aspiring women leaders needed support and training: 'They need assertiveness training. They also need confidence building and being told, "You can do it too". And I think that's the bottom line. And it's just showing that you can do it.'

Summary of Key Factors
Repeated listenings to the narratives of participants in this study led to the iden- tification of five Key Factors facilitative of the development and acquisition of leadership skills among women leaders from rural areas of Northern Ireland: Supportive People, Education, Leadership Training and Practical Experience, Setting and Achieving Goals, and Confidence. Supportive People were identified as family members (both family of origin and the women's current partner/ spouse and children), mentors and other beneficial relationships developed either informally or through purposeful networking. Participants articulated the indis- pensability of Education to leadership on three levels, relating it not only to the acquisition of personal leadership skills, but also to the development of commu- nity and governmental leadership as well. Leadership Training and Practical Experience were intertwined in many of the women's narratives, with a heavier emphasis being placed on the attainment of practical experience. This practical experience came in many forms, the three most significant being: participation in community, youth, religious and/or women's organizations; leadership during their student years in educational institutions and sport; and in their current employment roles. The fourth Key Factor – Setting and Achieving Goals – consisted of having a vision of what they wanted to achieve; persistence in pursu- ing that goal; and openness to unexpected means of achieving the goal or, in some situations, modifying the goal. The final Key Factor, Confidence (Belief in Self), went beyond the presentation of the women's verbalized self-confidence in the findings chapter to encompass participants' recommendations for confidence- building measures as tools for developing leadership among rural women. Each of these Key Factors emerged as contributing positively to the leadership develop- ment of the women in this study. Further, participants also cited the Key Factors as Crucial Supports for rural women aspiring to leadership.

4.4 Reconnection with Literature

Many of the findings were in agreement with extant literature addressing the position of women rural women and women in leadership. Specifically, resonance with academic literature was noted at points in each of the following areas: gender identity and roles, legitimization of non-participation, leadership as an elusive concept, the role of family in leadership development, the dual necessity of training and practical experience, and rural women's organizations as an entry point to wider community involvement. However, the findings deviated from current literature regarding the role of organizations in leadership development.

4.4.1 Gender identity and roles

The valuing of traditional gender identities and roles in rural communities (Silvasti, 2003) was apparent in this study in the narratives of several women. The caring tone present in many of the women's descriptions of their personal leadership styles appeared to stem from a desire to be perceived as nurturing. This corresponded with assertions by Heather *et al.* (2005) and Saugeres (2002) that women's acceptance in the rural community may be based on their ability to under-prioritize self-care, and that this is seen as a normal facet of family life.[17]

4.4.2 Legitimization of non-participation

Many participants rejected feminism and the label 'feminist'. This was often strongest at points where they spoke in voices that simultaneously affirmed both feminist principles and (conversely) gender roles that could be perceived as oppressive. These women expressed perceptions of feminism as negative, anti-men and/ or anti-family. Rather than being purely reactionary on their part, however, this rejection of feminism and 'feminist' signified the choice of non-participation in the feminist movement as a powerful means of asserting their identity as rural women. Therefore, these women affirm Shortall's (2008, p. 452) characterization of such choices as 'valid and legitimate . . . made from a position of power'.

4.4.3 Leadership as an elusive concept

There exists a multiplicity of works on leaders and leadership, each of which theorizes the concepts in its own unique way (among those cited in this study, see especially Uhl-Bien, 2006, and Ladkin, 2010). Section 1.4 in Chapter 1 of this work addressed the concept of leadership, and recognized the lack of authoritative definitions for the terms 'leader' and 'leadership'. Barker (2001) noted that the elusive quality of these definitions has led to increasingly complex and adaptable theories of leadership. The women in this study reflected this quandary by articulating a spectrum of perspectives from which they defined leadership and themselves as leaders.

4.4.4 The role of family in leadership development

As stated at several points throughout this book, the role of family in participants' leadership development was a crucial one. This is in obvious agreement with Avolio *et al.*'s (2009) work. His proposal of the family as a primary source of confidence building leading to the taking up of leadership positions found resonance with nearly all of the participants in the study. The findings were also deeply reflective of Daly and Dowds' (2005) depiction of Northern Ireland as a region with a particularly strong culture of seeking support from family.

4.4.5 The dual necessity of training and practical experience

Although participants advocated practical experience as the most effective means of gaining leadership skills, they portrayed both practical experience and leadership training as necessary for leadership development. Grint (2007) noted this both/and approach as important to leadership development. Further, he connected this dual approach to the ability to identify and utilize the positive aspects of any circumstance – another concept repeatedly voiced and practised by the participants.

4.4.6 Rural women's organizations and community involvement

Many participants were involved with Northern Ireland's Rural Women's Networks. Through their affiliation with these networks, they had been exposed to a variety of other community and regional organizations. That exposure then facilitated their involvement in activities outside their initial point of contact at the local network. In this way, the women's narratives confirmed Shortall's (2008) claim that involvement in Northern Ireland's Women's Networks also results in increased participation in other community activities.

4.4.7 The role of organizations in leadership development

Helen, Patricia and Veronica's narratives stood out from current literature by their portrayal of the organizations for which they worked as supportive to women and women's leadership development. Many organizations have been characterized as failing to address gender issues in ways that meaningfully affect their everyday practices (Kreimer, 2004; Westenholz *et al.*, 2006). However, Helen, Patricia and Veronica perceived their current employers as doing just that. Helen spoke of the active support she received from her political party. She credited that support with freeing her from having to waste energy fighting 'anti-women' and 'misogyny'. Patricia also recognized her employing organization as providing support to women through offering such options as flexible working hours, sick leave and part-time work. Finally, Veronica's work contrasted with the literature stating that women who choose to take time off to care for children would probably be excluded from higher levels in their organization (Truman, 1996). Her organization faced the unique challenge of a middle management comprised entirely of women in their childbearing years. Having herself reached a high level within the organization, she was utilizing her position to create policies allowing the women to 'go off and have their babies in comfort'. In the lived experiences of these three women, organizations had provided positive support rather than creating barriers to leadership.

Summary: Chapter 4

As a means of hearing the ways in which participants themselves identified and defined positive factors in their leadership development, their own voices were given precedence in the analysis of data. Careful listening and re-listening allowed for the identification of four External Factors (people, organizations and events) and nine Internal Factors (thought processes and choices). Further examination of these factors facilitated the recognition of five Key Factors and Crucial Supports that emerged as most significant in the women's responses and through their recommendations for aspiring rural women leaders. Each of these factors deeply impacted the participants' lives, and provided insight into the types of developmental activities and support to be encouraged among rural women aspiring to leadership.

Conclusions

This exploration of factors facilitating the development and acquisition of leadership skills among women from rural areas has examined the ways in which people, organizations and/or events supported the participants' evolution as leaders. Further, it endeavoured to discover what thought processes and choices participants exercised in order to overcome obstacles in their leadership development. Although these obstacles should *in no way* be minimized, the primary focus here was on *positive* factors contributing to leadership development among rural women in Northern Ireland.

This book has demonstrated the validity of two important observations regarding positive factors in leadership development: first, that rural women can, and do, enter leadership in spite of the many obstacles they face; and, secondly, that rural women are a powerful force for positive change in their own communities and beyond. These two observations intersected in the Key Factors identified by the study, which were formed not only by the women's narratives of their own leadership journeys, but also by their advice to – and hopes of support for – future rural women leaders. These Key Factors were: Supportive People, Education, Leadership Training and Practical Experience, Setting and Achieving Goals, and Confidence.

The utilization of a voice-centred relational method of analysis for this study provided a wealth of important data. This, in turn, gave rise to the question of the applicability of large-scale quantitative studies to local contexts and reinforced feminist concerns with the masking or silencing of vital sources of information in the form of women's voices. While large quantitative studies are important to on-going research and policy-making efforts, it is my assertion that localized, comparative cross-national and cross-regional qualitative studies should be undertaken to further elucidate ways in which rural women can be supported in their leadership development. Through such studies, mutually beneficial practices may be discovered and networks of support could be formed (see Bock, 2010a).

As noted in the book's introduction, the position of rural women is currently of particular interest to policy makers and international governing bodies. Additionally, the results of this study have clearly shown that rural women are quite capable of acting as leaders and articulating their own interests. For rural women to take up roles in decision-making bodies, they will require support in the form of policies that take into account their particular situations – not as 'non-urban', but as positively and uniquely rural. This may include the provision of training in policy making, political systems and advocacy. However, it should also be recognized that many rural women deeply value their localized realm of influence. Therefore, policy should also take into account the crucial contributions of rural women's networks and community organizations in improving the lives not only of rural women, but of rural men and children as well. This is particularly critical in terms of funding support for long-term projects, the administration of which would provide leadership opportunities and experience for rural women.

Secondly, policies addressing gender equality in all areas are still greatly needed. In spite of the on-going implementation of legislation such as Northern Ireland's *Section 75*, rural women continue to experience barriers to leadership through well-documented concerns such as childcare and the availability of flexible working arrangements. Policy makers would do well to take note of the ways in which organizations that meaningfully enact supportive policies and procedures positively influence developing leaders; and to draft policies that would encourage the continuation and expansion of such practices as well as creating means of sharing them with other organizations.

The importance of education in the development of rural women's leadership skills cannot be overestimated. Therefore, a third policy need is the mainstreaming of leadership training and confidence-building programmes at every level of education. Such policies should incorporate a broad definition of leadership, making use of its multi-faceted and diverse variants as a means of ensuring inclusivity. Additionally, policies of this nature should encourage the practical application of attained skills within the local community as a means of creating viable options to outmigration.

Finally, the women who participated in this research expressed in vibrant vocal panoply their passionate commitment to the advancement of rural women. It is my sincere hope that this work honours their voices and contributes to that advancement. It is also my hope that the positive focus of this research will be a catalyst for others to incorporate the exploration and reinforcement of positive aspects of rural life into research and policies concerning rural people.

End Notes

1. Although there is an invaluable body of literature addressing rural women in leadership in developing countries, the literature noted here is more directly connected, sociologically, with the cultural context of the women who participated in this study.

2. Emphasis on particular words and phrases is noted in two ways throughout the presentation of data: **bold** for briefly stated words with a slightly louder vocalization, and *italic* for words that are stretched for emphasis.

3. Brubaker and Cooper (2000) have problematized the usage of the term 'identity' in such contexts, claiming that overuse and incorrect usage mandate alternative terminology if 'identity' is to retain any useful meaning as a concept. Further, they juxtapose 'identity' with 'identification', thereby claiming to avoid the silencing of differences between and among groups of individuals by positing 'identity' as a label imposed from without and 'identification' as a process of internal significance to the person doing the self-identifying (p. 17). Brubaker and Cooper also reject 'identity' as an appropriate category from which to conduct analysis, claiming that 'conceptual clarity' (p. 36) can only be achieved through distinguishing 'identity' (which they see as constant and underlying) from 'self-understanding' (which they are willing to allow may be changeable) (p. 9). In the case of this study, however, their conceptualization of 'identity' as constant is reflective of at least three distinct identities common to the women in this study: rural, woman and leader. The participants' articulations of these three distinct identities are treated in detail in Section 2.4 of this book.

4. Morris and Evans describe *Farmers' Weekly* as 'the most significant farming publication in the UK' (p. 375).

5. Northern Ireland falls well within Pini's estimation, with a recent study showing that only 37% of managers and/or senior officials in Northern Ireland are women (Department of Enterprise, Trade and Investment, 2007).

6. The usage of the term 'identity' as a category of analysis has not been without contestation. See note 3, above.

7. Preliminary contact was established through attendance at meetings involving a number of women's groups throughout Northern Ireland. This had a snowball effect as I met women who were interested in participating in the study, or knew of others who might be.

8. In the interest of reflexive disclosure, it should be noted that, as the daughter of a rural family, these areas have proven formational in my own life, and thus my own life experience played a role in choosing these 'starting points'.

9. Note Katherine's words: 'I mean, I'm not-', leaving the listener to surmise from the broader context of her narrative what she was 'not-'. Namely: a feminist.

10. The 11+ was a placement exam given to primary school children, which determined their future schooling prospects and university path. The exam is no longer given in Northern Ireland.

11. In addition to providing information regarding the participants, the case studies also present exercises of reflexivity undertaken as a portion of the first step of the methodology. Within that context, I speak in my own voice, giving the reader the opportunity to identify the ways in which my voice shaped the analysis and presentation of the data (Gilligan *et al.*, 2003).

12. For the sake of anonymity, this participant will be identified as 'Alice'.

13. Throughout the text, 'L' in the context of quotations will refer to Lori, the author.

14. For the sake of anonymity, the participant will be identified as 'Doreen'.

15. The concept of positivity as used in this case study is taken from *Strengths Quest* by Donald O. Clifton, PhD and Edward 'Chip' Anderson, PhD. Their definition includes two phrases that aptly summarize Doreen's attitude: 'always on the lookout for the positive in the situation' (p. 64) and 'can't quite escape [the] conviction that it is good to be alive' (p. 65) (Clifton and Anderson, 2002).

16. For a more in-depth portrayal of Doreen's Positivity, please refer to Section 3.2.4.

17. It should be noted that one participant (Niamh) stood out by her reshaping of this nurturance. Her adamant dedication to feminism resulted in a recommendation that women care for themselves – even at the expense of family structures.

References

Adkins, L. and Lury, C., 1992. Gender and the labour market: old theory for new? In: H. Hinds, A. Phoenix and J. Stacey, eds, *Working Out: New Directions for Women's Studies*. London: Falmer Press, pp. 173–183

Alston, M., 2003. Women's representation in an Australian rural context. *Sociologia Ruralis*, **43**, 474–487

Appelbaum, S.H., Audet, L. and Miller, J.C., 2003. Gender and leadership? Leadership and gender? A journey through the landscape of theories. *Leadership & Organization Development Journal*, **24**(1/2), 43

Auerbach, J., Blum, L., Smith, V. and Williams, C., 1985. On Gilligan's "In a different voice". *Feminist Studies*, **11**(1), pp. 149–161

Avolio, B.J., Rotundo, M. and Walumbwa, F.O., 2009. Early life experiences as determinants of leadership role occupancy: the importance of parental influence and rule breaking behavior. *The Leadership Quarterly*, **20**(3), 329–342

Awbrey, S.M., 2007. The dynamics of vertical and horizontal diversity in organization and society. *Human Resource Development Review*, **6**(1), 7–32

Barker, R., 2001. The nature of leadership. *Human Relations*, **54**(4), 469–494

Bartky, S., 1993. Foucault, femininity and the modernisation of patriarchal power. In: S. Jackson, ed., *Women's Studies: Essential Readings*. New York: New York University Press, pp. 227–230

Beaulieu, L.J., 2005. Breaking walls, building bridges: expanding the presence and relevance of rural sociology. *Rural Sociology*, **70**(1), 1–27

Bell, M.M., Lloyd, S.E. and Vatovec, C., 2010. Activating the countryside: rural power, the power of the rural and the making of rural politics. *Sociologia Ruralis*, **50**(3), 205–224

Bennett, K., 2004. A time for change? Patriarchy, the former coalfields and family farming. *Sociologia Ruralis*, **44**(2), 147–166

Berik, G., 1996. Understanding the gender system in rural turkey: fieldwork dilemmas of conformity and intervention. In: D.L. Wolf, ed., *Feminist Dilemmas in Fieldwork*. Oxford: Westview Press, pp. 56–71

Bochner, A.P., 2001. Narrative's virtues. *Qualitative Inquiry,* **7**(2), 131–157

Bock, B.B., 2004. Fitting in and multi-tasking: Dutch farm women's strategies in rural entrepreneurship. *Sociologia Ruralis,* **44**(3), 245–260

Bock, B.B., 2006. Rurality and gender identity: an overview. In: Bock, B.B. and Shortall, S., eds, *Rural Gender Relations: Issues and Case Studies,* 1st edn. Wallingford: CAB International, pp. 279–287

Bock, B.B., 2010a. *Comparative Analysis and the Future of Rural Development Research.* PowerPoint Presentation edn. Wageningen: Wageningen University.

Bock, B.B., 2010b. *Personal and Social Development of Women in Rural Areas of Europe.* IP/B?AGRI/IC/2010_089. Brussels: European Parliament.

Bock, B.B. and De Haan, H., 2004. Rural gender studies in the Netherlands. In: H. Goverde, H. De Haan and M. Baylina, eds, *Power and Gender in European Rural Development.* Hants: Ashgate Publishing Limited, pp. 106–126

Bono, J.E., Shen, W. and Snyder, M., 2010. Fostering integrative community leadership. *The Leadership Quarterly,* **21**(2), 324–335

Bourdieu, P., 2003. Participant objectivation. *Journal of the Royal Anthropological Institute,* **9**, 281–294

Brandth, B., 1994. Changing femininity: the social construction of women farmers in Norway. *Sociologia Ruralis,* **34**(2–3), 127–149

Brandth, B., 1995. Rural masculinity in transition: gender images in tractor advertisements. *Journal of Rural Studies,* **11**(2), 123–133

Brandth, B., 2002. Gender identity in European family farming: a literature review. *Sociologia Ruralis,* **42**(3), 181–200

Brandth, B. and Haugen, M.S., 1997. Rural women, feminism and the politics of identity. *Sociologia Ruralis,* **37**(3), 325–344

Breitenbach, E. and Galligan, Y., 2004. *Gender Equality Indicators for Northern Ireland: a Discussion Document.* Belfast, Northern Ireland: Office of the First Minister and Deputy First Minister.

Brewer, J.D., 2000. *Ethnography.* Buckingham: Open University Press.

Brooks, A., 2007. Feminist standpoint epistemology: building knowledge and empowerment through women's lived experience. In: S.N. Hesse-Biber and P.L. Leavy, eds, *Feminist Research Practice: a Primer.* Thousand Oaks: Sage Publications, pp. 53–82

Brubaker, R. and Cooper, F., 2000. Beyond "identity". *Theory and Society,* **29**(1), pp. 1–47

Buch, E.D. and Staller, K.M., 2007. The feminist practice of ethnography. In: S.N. Hesse-Biber and P.L. Leavy, eds, *Feminist Research Practice: a Primer.* Thousand Oaks: Sage Publications, pp. 187–221

Byrne, B., 2003. Reciting the self: narrative representations of the self in qualitative interviews. *Feminist Theory,* **4**(1), 29–49

Clifton, D.O. and Anderson, E.C., 2002. *Strengths Quest: Discover and Develop your Strengths in Academics, Career, and Beyond.* Washington, DC: The Gallup Organization.

Cloke, P., 1997. Country backwater to virtual village? Rural studies and 'the cultural turn'. *Journal of Rural Studies,* **13**(4), 367–375

Cloke, P. and Milbourne, P., 1992. Deprivation and lifestyles in rural Wales. II. Rurality and the cultural dimension. *Journal of Rural Studies,* **8**(4), 359–371

Conner, J.O. and Strobel, K., 2007. Leadership development. An examination of individual and programmatic growth. *Journal of Adolescent Research,* **22**(3), 275–297

Connolly, P., 2005. Summary – "It Goes Without Saying (Well, Sometimes)": Racism, Whiteness and Identity in Northern Ireland. Belfast, Northern Ireland: Online Research Bank – a constituent part of ARK.

Cosslett, T., Easton, A. and Summerfield, P., eds, 1996. *Women, Power and Resistance: an Introduction to Women's Studies.* Buckingham: Open University Press.

Crawley, M., 2005. Position Paper – Sustaining the Work of the Women's Sector in Rural Areas. Belfast: Women's Resource and Development Agency.

Crowley, H. and Himmelweit, S., eds, 1992. *Knowing Women: Feminism and Knowledge.* Cambridge: Polity in association with the Open University.

Cunningham, M., 2008. Influences of gender ideology and housework allocation on women's employment over the life course. *Social Science Research,* **37**(1), 254–267

Daly, M. and Dowds, L., 2005. *Final Report on Project R000223682 Family and Social Networks in Northern Ireland.* R000223682. Swindon: Economic and Social Research Council.

Day, D.V., 2000. Leadership development: a review in context. *The Leadership Quarterly,* **11**(4), 581–613

Delphy, C., 1984. *Close to Home.* London: Hutchinson.

Department of Enterprise, Trade and Investment, 2007. *Labour Market Statistics Bulletin: Women in Northern Ireland.* Belfast, Northern Ireland: National Statistics, Northern Ireland Statistics and Research Agency.

Elliott, C. and Stead, V., 2008. Learning from leading women's experience: towards a sociological understanding. *Leadership,* **4**(2), 159–180

Emirbayer, M., 1997. Manifesto for a relational sociology. *American Journal of Sociology,* **103**(2), 281

European Forum: The Role of Women in Sustainable Development of the Rural Environment, 2010. *Recommendations of the Technical Seminar – European Forum: Women in the Sustainable Development of the Rural World,* 27–29 April, 2010, pp. 1–4

Farmar-Bowers, Q., 2010. Understanding the strategic decisions women make in farming families. *Journal of Rural Studies,* **26**(2), 141–151

Finch, J., 1996. Women, 'the' family and families. In: T. Cosslett, A. Easton and P. Summerfield, eds, *Women, Power and Resistance: an Introduction to Women's Studies.* Buckingham: Open University Press, pp. 13–22

Flax, J., 1987. Postmodernism and gender relations in feminist theory. *Signs,* **12**(4, Within and Without: Women, Gender, and Theory), 621–643

Fonow, M.M. and Cook, J.A., 2005. Feminist methodology: new applications in the academy and public policy. *Signs: Journal of Women in Culture and Society,* **30**(4), 2211–2236

Ford, J., 2005. Examining leadership through critical feminist readings. *Journal of Health Organization and Management,* **19**(3), 236–251

Gardner, G., 2001. Unreliable memories and other contingencies: problems with biographical knowledge. *Qualitative Research,* **1**(2), 185–204

Gilligan, C., Spencer, R., Weinberg, M.K. and Bertsch, T., 2003. On the *Listening Guide*: a voice-centered relational method. In: P.M. Camic, J.E. Rhodes and L. Yardley, eds, *Qualitative Research in Psychology: Expanding Perspectives in Methodology and Design.* Washington, DC: American Psychological Association, pp. 157–172

Greenberg, H.M. and Sweeney, P.J., 2005. Leadership: qualities that distinguish women. *Financial Executive,* **21**(6), 32

Grimshaw, J., 1993. Autonomy and identity in feminist thinking. In: S. Jackson, ed., *Women's Studies: Essential Readings.* New York: New York University Press, pp. 42–44

Grint, K., 2007. Learning to lead: can Aristotle help us find the road to wisdom? *Leadership,* **3**(2), 231–246

Hackman, M.Z. and Johnson, C.E., 2000. *Leadership: a Communication Perspective,* 3rd edn. Prospect Heights: Waveland Press.

Hatch, M.J., 1997. *Organization Theory: Modern, Symbolic, and Postmodern Perspectives*. New York: Oxford University Press.

Heather, B., Skillen, L., Young, J. and Vladicka, T., 2005. Women's gendered identities and the restructuring of rural Alberta. *Sociologia Ruralis*, **45**(1), 86–97

Henig, R., 1996. Women and political power in Britain in the 1990s. In: T. Cosslett, A. Easton and P. Summerfield, eds, *Women, Power and Resistance: an Introduction to Women's Studies*. Buckingham: Open University Press, pp. 263–271

Hesse-Biber, S.N., 2007. The practice of feminist in-depth interviewing. In: S.N. Hesse-Biber and P.L. Leavy, eds, *Feminist Research Practice: a Primer*. Thousand Oaks: Sage Publications, pp. 111–148

Howell, S.L., Carter, V.K. and Schied, F.M., 2002. Gender and women's experience at work: a critical and feminist perspective on human resource development. *Adult Education Quarterly*, **52**(2), 112–127

Hughes, A., Morris, C. and Seymour, S., eds, 2000. *Ethnography and Rural Research*. Cheltenham: The Countryside & Community Press.

Jack, D.C., 1991. *Silencing the Self: Women and Depression*. New York: Harper Perennial.

Jackson, A.Y., 2004. Performativity identified. *Qualitative Inquiry*, **10**(5), 673–690

Jackson, S., ed., 1993. *Women's Studies: Essential Readings*. New York: University Press.

Katz, C., 1996. The expeditions of conjurers: ethnography, power, and pretense. In: D.L. Wolf, ed., *Feminist Dilemmas in Fieldwork*. Oxford: Westview Press, pp. 170–184

Keith, K. and Malone, P., 2005. Housework and the wages of young, middle-aged, and older workers. *Contemporary Economic Policy*, **23**(2), 224

Kelly, R. and Shortall, S., 2002. 'Farmer' wives': women who are off-farm breadwinners and the implications for on-farm gender relations. *Journal of Sociology*, **38**(4), 327–343

Kreimer, M., 2004. Labour market segregation and the gender-based division of labour. *European Journal of Women's Studies*, **11**(2), 223–246

Kvale, S., 2006. Dominance through interviews and dialogues. *Qualitative Inquiry*, **12**(3), 480–500

Ladkin, D., 2010. *Rethinking Leadership: a New Look at Old Leadership Questions*, 1st edn. Cheltenham: Edward Elgar Publishing Limited.

Lal, J., 1996. Situating locations: the politics of self, identity, and "other". In: D.L. Wolf, ed., *Feminist Dilemmas in Fieldwork*. Oxford: Westview Press, pp. 185–214

Lather, P., 2001. Postbook: working the ruins of feminist ethnography. *Signs*, **27**(1), 199–227

Lawler, S., 1996. Motherhood and identity. In: T. Cosslett, A. Easton and P., Summerfield, eds, *Women, Power and resistance: an Introduction to Women's Studies*. Buckingham: Open University Press, pp. 153–164

LeCompte, M.D., 2002. The transformation of ethnographic practice: past and current challenges. *Qualitative Research*, **2**(3), 283–299

Leonard, P., 2002. Organizing gender? Looking at metaphors as frames of meaning in gender/organizational texts. *Gender, Work & Organization*, **9**, 60–80

Letherby, G., 2004. Reply to Ann Oakley. *Sociology*, **38**, 193–194

Little, J., 2002. *Gender and Rural Geography: Identity, Sexuality and Power in the Countryside*. Essex: Pearce Education Limited.

Little, J., 2007. Constructing nature in the performance of rural heterosexualities. *Environment and Planning D: Society and Space*, **25**(5), 851

Little, J. and Austin, P., 1996. Women and the rural idyll. *Journal of Rural Studies*, **12**(2), 101–111

Little, J. and Panelli, R., 2003. Gender research in rural geography. *Gender Place and Culture – Journal of Feminist Geography,* **10**(3), 281–290

Macaulay, T. and Laverty, B., 2007. *Baseline Study of Rural Women's Infrastructure in Northern Ireland.* Cookstown, Co. Tyrone, Northern Ireland: Rural Community Network and the Rural Women's Sectoral Programme Consortium.

Mahon, M., 2007. New populations; shifting expectations: The changing experience of Irish rural space and place. *Journal of Rural Studies,* **23**(3), 345–356

Maleta, Y., 2009. Playing with fire. *Journal of Sociology,* **45**(3), 291–306

Mauthner, N.S. and Doucet, A., 2003. Reflexive accounts and accounts of reflexivity in qualitative data analysis. *Sociology,* **37**(3), 413–431

McAlister, S., Gray, A.M. and Neill, G., 2007. *Still Waiting: the Stories Behind the Statistics of Young Women Growing up in Northern Ireland.* Belfast, Northern Ireland: Youth Action Northern Ireland.

McAreavey, R., 2008. Researcher and employee: reflections on reflective practice in rural development research. *Sociologia Ruralis,* **48**(4), 389–407

McCall, L., 2005. The complexity of intersectionality. *Signs: Journal of Women in Culture and Society,* **30**(3), 1771–1800

McCormack, C., 1993. Nature, culture and gender: a critique. In: S. Jackson, ed., *Women's Studies: Essential Readings.* New York: New York University Press, pp. 84–86

McNay, L., 1999. Gender and narrative identity. *Journal of Political Ideologies,* **4**(3), 315–336

McNay, L., 2003. Agency, anticipation and indeterminacy in feminist theory. *Feminist Theory,* **4**, 139–148

McNay, L., 2004. Agency and experience: gender as a lived relation. *The Sociological Review,* **52**, 173–190

Mills, A.J., 2002. Studying the gendering of organizational culture over time: concerns, issues and strategies. *Gender, Work & Organization,* **9**, 286–307

Morris, C. and Evans, N., 2001. 'Cheese makers are always women': gendered representations of farm life in the agricultural press. *Gender, Place and Culture,* **8**, 375–390

Mutch, A., Delbridge, R. and Ventresca, M., 2006. Situating organizational action: the relational sociology of organizations. *Organization,* **13**(5), 607–626

Naples, N.A., 2000. Standpoint epistemology and the use of self-reflection in feminist ethnography: Lessons for rural sociology. *Rural Sociology,* **65**(2), 194

Naples, N.A. and Sachs, C., 2000. Standpoint epistemology and the uses of self-reflection in feminist ethnography: lessons for rural sociology. *Rural Sociology,* **65**, 194–214

Northern Ireland Department of Agriculture and Rural Development, 2006. *DARD Rural Strategy 2007–2013.* Belfast: DARD.

O'Hara, P., 1994. Out of the shadows. Women on family farms and their contribution to agriculture and rural development. In: M. Van De Burg and M. Endeveld, eds, *Women on Family Farms. Gender Research, EC Policies and New Perspectives.* Wageningen: Wageningen University, pp. 49–66

Oliver, D.G., Serovich, J.M. and Mason, T.L., 2005. Constraints and opportunities with interview transcription: towards reflection in qualitative research. *Social Forces,* **84**(2), 1273–1289

Parker, M., 2000. The sociology of organizations and the organization of sociology: some reflections on the making of a division of labour. *The Sociological Review,* **48**(1), 124–146

Perrow, C., 2000. An organizational analysis of organizational theory. *Contemporary Sociology,* **29**(3), 469–476

Pillow, W., 2003. Confession, catharsis, or cure? Rethinking the uses of reflexivity as methodological power in qualitative research. *International Journal of Qualitative Studies in Education*, **16**(2), 175

Pini, B., 2003a. Feminist methodology and rural research: reflections on a study of an Australian agricultural organisation. *Sociologia Ruralis*, **43**(4), 418–434

Pini, B., 2003b. 'We could have had the old girl out in the paddock years ago': widowed women, farming and agricultural leadership. *Work, Employment and Society*, **17**(1), 171–182

Pini, B., 2004a. Counting them in, not out: surveying farm women about agricultural leadership. *Geographical Research*, **42**(2), 249–260

Pini, B., 2004b. On being a nice country girl and an academic feminist: using reflexivity in rural social research. *Journal of Rural Studies*, **20**(2), 169–180

Pini, B., 2005. The third sex: women leaders in Australian agriculture. Gender – Work and Organization, **12**(1), 73–89

Ramazanoglu, C. and Holland, J., 2002. *Feminist Methodology: Challenges and Choices*. London: Sage Publications.

Reed, M., 2005. Reflections on the 'realist turn' in organization and management studies. *Journal of Management Studies*, **42**, 1621–1644

Reinharz, S. and Chase, S.E., 2002. Interviewing women. In: J.F. Gubrium and J.A. Holstein, eds, *Handbook of Interview Research: Context and Method*. Thousand Oaks: Sage Publications, pp. 221–238

Risman, B.J., 2004. Gender as a social structure: theory wrestling with activism. *Gender and Society*, **18**(4), 429–451

Roberts, B., 2002. *Biographical Research*. Buckingham: Open University Press.

Rosenberg, K. and Howard, J., 2008. Finding feminist sociology: a review essay. *Signs: Journal of Women in Culture and Society*, **33**(3), 675–696

Rural Women's Networks, Northern Ireland Rural Women's Network, 2007. *Response to Consultation on EU Programme for Peace and Reconciliation (Peace III) 2007–2013*. Cookstown: Northern Ireland Rural Women's Network.

Sachs, C., 1983. *The Invisible Farmers: Women in Agricultural Production*. Lanham: Rowman & Littlefield Publishers.

Sanday, P.R., 1993. *Female Power and Male Dominance: on the origins of sexual inequality*. New York: New York University Press, pp. 86–89

Saugeres, L., 2002. The cultural representation of the farming landscape: masculinity, power and nature. *Journal of Rural Studies*, **18**(4), 373–384

Scheurich, J.J., 1995. A postmodernist critique of research interviewing. *International Journal of Qualitative Studies in Education*, **8**(3), 239

Scott, W.R., 2004. Reflections on a half-century of organizational sociology. *Annual Review of Sociology*, **30**, 1–21

Shortall, S., 1999. *Women and Farming: Property and Power*. Basingstoke: Macmillan.

Shortall, S., 2001. Women in the field: women, farming and organizations. *Gender, Work & Organization*, **8**, 164–181

Shortall, S., 2002. Gendered agricultural and rural restructuring: a case study of Northern Ireland. *Sociologia Ruralis*, **42**(2), 160–175

Shortall, S., 2003. *Women in Rural Areas in Northern Ireland: a Policy Discussion Document Prepared for the Rural Community Network*. Cookstown: Rural Community Network.

Shortall, S., 2006. *Briefing Paper: Developing Gender Research in Rural Scotland*. Inverness: UHIPolicyWeb.

Shortall, S., 2008. Are rural development programmes socially inclusive? Social inclusion, civic engagement, participation, and social capital: exploring the differences. *Journal of Rural Studies,* **24**(4), 450–457

Silvasti, T., 2003. Bending borders of gendered labour division on farms: the case of Finland. *Sociologia Ruralis,* **43**, 154–166

Smart, C., 2009. Shifting horizons: reflections on qualitative methods. *Feminist Theory,* **10**(3), 295–308

Solansky, S.T., 2010. The evaluation of two key leadership development program components: leadership skills assessment and leadership mentoring. *The Leadership Quarterly,* **21**(4), 675–681

Stack, C.B., 1996. Writing Ethnography: Feminist Critical Practice. In: D.L. Wolf, ed., *Feminist Dilemmas in Fieldwork.* Oxford: Westview Press, pp. 96–106

Trinidad, C. and Normore, A.H., 2005. Leadership and gender: a dangerous liaison? *Leadership & Organization Development Journal,* **26**(7/8), 574–591

Truman, C., 1996. Paid work in women's lives: continuity and change. In: T. Cosslett, A. Easton and P. Summerfield, eds, *Women, Power and Resistance: an Introduction to Women's Studies.* Buckingham: Open University Press, pp. 35–44

Uhl-Bien, M., 2006. Relational leadership theory: exploring the social processes of leadership and organizing. *The Leadership Quarterly,* **17**, 654

Walby, S., 2001. Against epistemological chasms: the science question in feminism revisited. *Signs,* **26**(2), 485–509

Walsh, J.P., Meyer, A.D. and Schoonhoven, C.B., 2006. A future for organization theory: living in and living with changing organizations. *Organization Science,* **17**(5), 657–672

Westenholz, A., Pedersen, J.S. and Dobbin, F., 2006. Introduction: institutions in the making: identity, power, and the emergence of new organizational forms. *American Behavioral Scientist,* **49**(7), 889–896

Wilkinson, J. and Blackmore, J., 2008. Re-presenting women and leadership: a methodological journey. *International Journal of Qualitative Studies in Education,* **21**(2), 123–136

Wolf, D.L., 1996. Situating feminist dilemmas in fieldwork. In: D.L. Wolf, ed., *Feminist Dilemmas in Fieldwork.* Oxford: Westview Press, pp. 1–55

Women's Resource and Development Agency, 2008. *Women and the Conflict: Talking about the "Troubles" and Planning for the Future.* Belfast: Women's Resource and Development Agency; Women's Centres Regional Partnership.

Index